山與海的職日生

一頭一城一職一人一誌一

連明偉——著

Stories around Toucheng

推薦序

扎根於生活的文化底蘊

—— 國家發展委員會主任委員・龔明鑫

「所有創作都需要靈感，同時，所有靈感都必須扎根於生活。」

〈低調的豐足──藍文萬〉

地方創生是一個長期耕耘的推動過程，透過在地 DNA 的發掘與公部門的協力，才能塑造獨具特色的地方產業。在宜蘭頭城有一群人，他們用自己的工作所長在當地發光發熱，有土生土長的當地人，退休移居的新成員，也有從地球的另一端來的外國人，融合了當地山與海的素材，用各自的手藝，讓這個小鎮充滿著藝術氛圍和生命力，讓頭城在地文化藝術更加多元及璀璨。

本書特別將職人定義為「居住頭城，對自己的產品、作品或是所做的事情引以為傲、在地深耕許久，且和頭城在地文化、土地有連結」，描述了一個專屬於頭城的職人誌，創作團隊撰述當地 30 位職人在地奮鬥的動人故事，刻劃職人對於理念的展現。

有職人本身原從事買賣行業，因對於拼布藝術嗜好，從自己的興趣中培育出自

身另一項技能；也有遠從南非來的外國遊客，因深愛頭城地區的海浪，留在臺灣將自己手工製作衝浪板的技藝在宜蘭傳承下去，更有年輕人承接北管文化，凝聚傳統而形塑出新時代的頭城風貌。30 篇的職人故事，除了讓讀者對於頭城的人文風貌有更深刻的了解外，更是頭城地區地方創生的繁星成果展現。

　　政府推動地方創生已有數年，在全臺各地，有更多職人的故事，同時也是地方創生的故事，透過地方創生的持續推動，包含設立全臺74 座青年培力工作站，實質鼓勵在地蹲點經營的創生青年，建立支持系統陪伴輔導青年落地扎根，開創地方創生事業。同時亦透過中興新村閒置空間活化再生，作為中臺灣創生培能平台，由專業營運團隊協助國內有意投入地方創生之團隊駐村發展，推動輔導、募資、獎勵，協助橋接國內外資源，促進跨領域合作。

　　期待未來，更多創生團隊們在培力後，能於各地開枝散葉，逐步開拓獨具特色的地方產業，持續煥發著生機，也正是這些扎根於生活的文化底蘊，值得你我細細品味。

頭城三十加二 英雄之旅的故事

——國立政治大學創造力講座名譽教授·吳靜吉

《山與海的職日生：頭城職人誌》是由彭仁鴻的蘭城巷弄有限公司統籌，得獎無數的頭城作家連明偉書寫的作品。 在「本書出版資訊」中開宗明義表示「能以觀光客作為使用者閱讀這本書，因此，它更是本旅遊書籍，希望以職人故事帶領大家旅遊頭城！」

這些職人是誰？為什麼他們的故事值得傑出作家書寫？又為什麼他們的故事可以帶領「觀光客」認識頭城？ 書中三十位職人加上統籌的彭仁鴻和書寫的連明偉之職涯追尋，都是一段段各異其趣的英雄之旅。

電影導演盧卡斯（George Lucas）在拍攝《星際大戰》面臨困境時，重讀大學翻過卻未深究的坎伯（Joseph Campbell）的《千面英雄》，他讀著讀著突然領悟所有的英雄都經過起程、啟蒙和回歸的歷程，熱情地呼應內心召喚、使命夢想。

人在清醒的生活中大約三分之一的時間都在工作，以色列心理學家 Tirza Willner 等人以五個角度分析人所以工作的理由。

我們可以借用這些工作取向來了解這三十加二位職人的工作意義。

有人把工作視為謀生或差事（job），既然工作只是差事、謀生的必需，只是為了打發時間、賺取生活費，以支持家庭和自己的生活方式，工作便成了非不得已，所以不小心就會得過且過、敷衍了事。

有人把工作當成事業（career），希望在未來的工作場所中獲得影響力和權力，經由努力和學習可以晉升到更高的職位，也願意承擔額外的職務和責任。

第三個工作取向是社會鑲嵌（social embeddedness）。偏重這種取向的人認為工作是尋求歸屬感的地方，希望能夠感受到工作場所愉快的人際關係，自己是團隊或組織內的一份子，是歡樂社交的情感連結。

有些人總是閒不下來，不工作就不知如何打發時間，在家無事可忙反而覺得無聊，他們可以忙中取樂，甚至忙碌成癮。這是第四種的忙碌工作取向。

第五種工作取向則把工作視為自我認同和追尋人生目標的召喚（calling），因為熱情追逐自己的使命和夢想，而展開英雄探險之旅。這樣的工作取向者認為工作賦予個人生命的意義，有機會使自己在乎的大小世界變得更美好，喜歡與同事分享工作的意義和創新，也喜歡與別人談論工作、歸屬和認同的行業和工作體驗等。

這三十加二位職人正是坎伯所稱的英雄。他們各自呼應內心召喚，克服各種困難，探險的旅途中因緣際會遇見良師益友，而逐漸實現自己選擇的目標和夢想，當然這裡所謂的英雄不分男女，也就是沒

有「Her」，「Hero」只剩下 0。

　　閱讀或傾聽這三十加二位「山與海的職日生」踏上英雄之旅的生命故事，不僅了解這些職人的生涯追尋，也借此體驗頭城的風土人情。

　　臺灣和世界許多國家一樣，都曾經瘋狂地尋找甚至建構創意城市，特別是在美國的 Richard Florida 教授於 2002 年出版《創意新貴》和英國 Charles Landry 於 2008 出版《創意城市》後。「官」、「學」、「文化」各界熱情地啟動了臺灣創意城市的發掘與建構。UNESCO 也在 2004 年建立全世界的創意城市網絡，評審美食、設計、電影、媒體藝術、文學、音樂、手工藝與民間藝術 7 個領域的創意城市。

　　美國農業部意外發現在離大都會不遠的一些鄉村小鎮，因為網路方便，吸引不少難以負擔高額房租與生活費用，並且嚮往自然綠色區域的創意工作人員，這些移居人運用各自的才情豐富了村里的風土人情。

　　頭城就是屬於這樣的鄉村小鎮，我認為好山好水、山海相看兩不厭的臺灣「創意城市」可以將之轉化為創意城「鄉」。

　　根據 Florida 的理論，創意城市通常都具備四個 T，分別是 Talent（人才）、Tolerance（包容）、Technology（科技）和 Territorial Assets（自然與人造的愉悅環境）。這三十加二位職人都是人才，橫跨 UNESCO 創意城市網絡中的六個領域（除了電影）。頭城的包容力展現在這三十加二位職人的背景，其中有土生土長的留鄉人、有返鄉青年，有本國新住民，也有來自外國取得本國籍的

新移民。自然環境的美麗和人造的舒適愉悅環境，充分顯現頭城Territorial Assets 的迷人之處，此時只有第四個 Technology，不是頭城創意城鄉特色，如果《山與海的職日生：頭城職人誌》能夠勾引科技軟體和包括電影在內的新舊媒體人才聚會頭城，頭城便是道地的創意城鄉。

　　這本著作雖然沒有彭仁鴻和連明偉的故事，兩人卻活生生地貫穿這 30 篇「山與海的職日生」的職人誌中，何況他們兩人的個別故事都在網路上閃閃發光。增加他們的故事讓好奇探索的觀光客更能體驗頭城的風土人情。

每個人的故鄉都是「獨一無二」的

── 電子時報董事長／社長・黃欽勇

有回看到現代史學大師湯恩比與日本史學家池田大作的對話。池田大作問湯恩比，如果讓您有選擇的話，您會希望在什麼時代，出生在什麼地方？

湯恩比說：「我希望在西元一世紀時，出生在新疆的疏勒」，池田大作心領神會。做為一個研究科技產業競合，談半導體與地緣政治的我而言，湯恩比的說法，給我很大的想像空間與深刻的體會。

新疆的疏勒，就是今天的喀什。西元一世紀時，羅馬帝國的文明從這裡走向了中土，而幾乎就在同一個時代，印度的佛教文化也從這裡走進了中國，甚至今天穿越巴基斯坦的中巴鐵路，也從這裡進入中國。喀什，人類文明的匯聚點，能在一世紀出生於喀什，對一個史學家而言是件多麼愉快，但又求之不得的奇遇！

但每個人的故鄉都是獨一無二的，從世俗的眼光來看，這是個平凡無奇的小鎮。2.8 萬的人口，小到很容易被遊客遺忘，甚至連北宜高速公路都只是「擦身而過」而已。但頭城人知道，近代到宜蘭開墾的閩

南移民多數從這裡上岸，而 1883 年烏石港淤塞與 1924 年山洪暴發兩次的滄海桑田，是時代的見證，也是我們傳承自老一代的老鎮記憶。第一次的淤塞在宜蘭舊河道形成河港（頭圍港），頭城也被指名為東海岸唯一的「正港」，也成為 19、20 世紀交替之際，宜蘭最富裕的工商小鎮，搶孤、大神尪也都是那個時代頭城人留給後代的共同記憶。

1924 年的山洪暴發，加上北宜鐵路通車，徹底改變了頭城以河港爭取到的工商地位，頭城慢慢走向沉寂，而這是將近 100 年的時空轉換。1930 年前後，日本殖民政府推動「市街改正」，幾棟巴洛克式的老建築，標誌著頭城過去曾有的繁華，而頭城的重心也從和平老街移往開蘭路。

高山蒼蒼，大海洋洋，登上海拔 1,000 公尺的頭城第一高峰「鶯仔嶺」，從高處遠望故鄉是種幸福的感覺。過去的開蘭小鎮文風鼎盛，孕育出許多詩人、書法家；現代的頭城不乏享譽產業、學術與醫界的拔尖人物。滄海桑田、物換星移，頭城是臺灣從農業時代走向工業時代的活歷史。

說不完的故事，講不完的家鄉軼事，就像諾貝爾獎得主泰戈爾的這句話：「不管樹影有多長，總是連著樹幹連著根！」

序

從文風小鎮到 Glocal 國際村的創生實踐
職人背影，頭城縮影，

——蘭城巷弄有限公司（金魚厝邊）執行長・彭仁鴻

以替代役薪資積蓄租下邱金魚老鎮長古厝，成立蘭城巷弄迄今七年，當初立下目標，要將小鎮能量帶向國際，讓大家的專業與才華都有更大的舞台可以發揮。

起初透過老街文化藝術季、市集、小旅行等活動，串聯在地居民、島內移民及外籍人才等社群，創造交流互動的機會，進而營造「好生活」支持系統。接著發覺「在頭城生活要如何創業、就業的問題」，開始規劃「創就業」的課程，如公司設立、財務、行銷、報稅等，希望將頭城形塑成宜居小鎮，重建地域品牌，這也是金魚厝邊存在的價值與意義。

說起來簡單，但在地方創生實踐過程中，大多數返鄉青年，無論是自行創業或承繼家業，都有實體商品營運。但金魚厝邊選擇以文化發展為主體，注定是一場硬仗，要苦撐，耐得住煎熬，無法得知何時開花結果，如同進行不見天日的下水道工程。我們沒有去想、也不敢去想「在有生之年能做到什麼程度？」只能往前衝，一生懸命去打拚。

　　七年蹲點努力，終於獲得肯定與鼓勵。很榮幸，金魚厝邊有機會承接主辦 2023 年 5 月的亞太社會創新高峰會，使沉靜的力量瞬間爆發，讓小鎮躍昇國際舞台，同時回應金魚厝邊在國發會青年培力工作站致力推動「Glocalization 在地化」與頭城國際地球村的使命。

　　金魚厝邊能堅持至今，歸根於接觸在地職人，看見他們頂真做事的態度，堅持到底的精神。點醒我們要將這樣的精神徹底發揮，將各種網絡關係交織連結起來，讓金魚厝邊成為提供在地諮詢服務的中介組織，目前的青年培力工作站就是具體的實現。

　　金魚厝邊早在 2018 年辦理老街藝術季《巷弄裡的草根生活》時，就曾串聯 100 家「頭城勁厝 Way」店家，帶領遊客一起找尋老街的草根生活與動人故事。深耕至今，我們有能力透過田野訪查，深度訪談 30 位職人，金魚厝邊不單單以老街旅遊為目的，更希望從文化教育、藝術工藝、在地產業、公眾環境四個大面向，介紹在地深耕、默默付出的職人生活，領域從山間、老街擴展到漁村，全面呈現頭城在地的面貌，這也是頭城生活的縮影。

　　《山與海職日生：頭城職人誌》由在地文學作家連明偉撰寫，細讀後會發現這本書以山海為背景，職人為核心，在雋永筆鋒下看見小鎮人才薈萃，臥虎藏龍。不但挖掘老記憶與老技藝，還記載新生代、新移民創就業的心路歷程，可當作人物誌，也可當作歷史書。在推展觀光旅遊之際，則可藉此書讓遊客深入了解頭城的文化內涵。

　　金魚厝邊從事地方創生，推動在地文化事業，更想藉由這本書向鄉親報告：小鎮因為這些職人，讓未來充滿生機與希望。

目錄

01 老街區

02 車站以南 94

03 車站以北 140

04 五漁村　　174

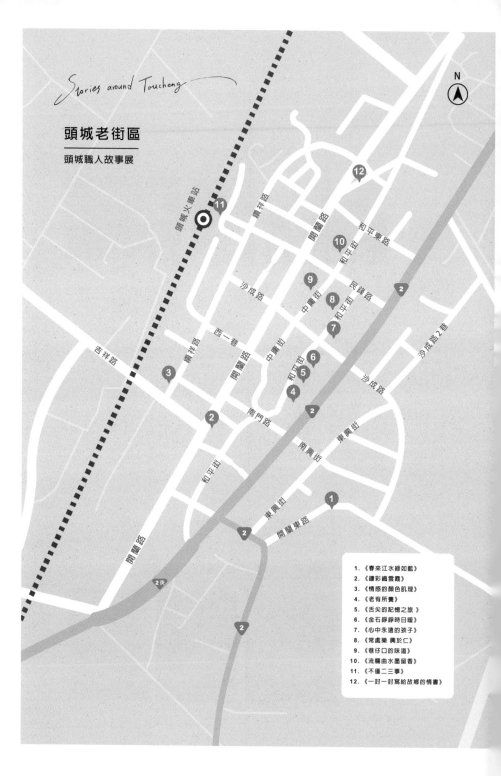

Stories around Toucheng

頭城老街區

頭城職人故事展

頭城火車站

吉祥路

嶺祥路

沙成路

西一巷

開蘭路

中廣街

和平街

南門路

南興街

東興街

開蘭路

和平東路

和平街

民鋒路

和平街

沙成路

沙成路2巷

開蘭東路

開蘭路

N

1. 《春來江水綠如藍》
2. 《鍵彩織雲霞》
3. 《情感的顏色肌理》
4. 《老有所養》
5. 《舌尖的記憶之旅》
6. 《金石錚錚時日暖》
7. 《心中永遠的孩子》
8. 《常處樂 興於仁》
9. 《巷仔口的味道》
10. 《流觴曲水墨留香》
11. 《不僅二三事》
12. 《一封一封寫給故鄉的情書》

老街區

Toucheng Old Street

從頭城火車站出來，往前行，過開蘭路後就到老街區，若是平常日抵達，安安靜靜是正常。可「按書索驥」找到店家，也不妨上網搜尋「頭城二三事」，或許會跳出意外的驚喜。

藝術工藝

春來江水綠如藍——喚醒藍染裁縫技藝・蔡秀惠

　　天空是藍的，大海是藍的，一叢一叢春秋花草也是藍的，濃淡輕沾，衣裾搖擺，浸潤整個故土。

　　蔡秀惠，1961 年生，專業裁縫師，開設「秀惠裁縫工作室」數年。提供的服務繁多精細，大至服裝設計，小至衣褲修補。原先專門製作婚嫁服飾，技術精湛，民眾口耳相傳夙負盛名。近年加入 105 年成立的「宜蘭染工坊發展協會」，參與宜蘭染藝技研習營，作品曾在蘭博的藍染展覽中展出。學習藍染，是為了精進染衣技術，不知不覺積累的多年經驗，替自己、鄉鎮與土地開啟一連串在地產業的迢遙歷史追尋。

　　1880 年清朝時期，臺灣的天然藍靛染料曾經盛極一時，高居外銷品第三，爾後德國拜耳化學公司的化學人造藍靛研製成功，藍染種植不再符合經濟成本，費時耗工，20 世紀初期藍染產業遂快速衰退，無以為繼，1940 年後已無人種植藍染植物。**藍染曾是宜蘭頭城的重要產業**，約 28 戶從事相關工作，和平街有多家染坊，如今，頭城老街只餘「源合成商號」一戶染坊老建築，可供懷想思量。

　　植物染色之中，只有藍色系得透過發酵還

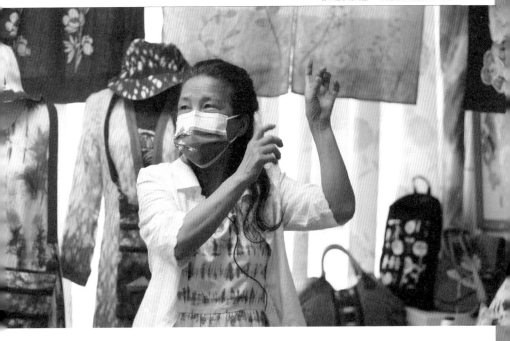

原法，才得以取得藍色素進行染色，而從植物萃取至取得染料，約得花上一至兩星期的工序期程。早期，頭城福德坑山區曾經種植大量的藍染植物，主要包含山藍（大菁）和木藍（小菁）。山藍喜陰，適合植於背陽山坡；木藍好陽，多栽植平地河床。頭城與礁溪的自然環境，正好符合藍染植物的生存條件。

　　一個被遺忘的產業，一個值得被喚醒的沉睡經濟活動，一個隱藏先人歷史與文化脈絡的日常生活，數年之後捲土重來，以復甦記憶的新型文創形式，重新回到現代。

　　蔡秀惠表示，礁溪、宜蘭、羅東乃至臺灣其他藍染重鎮，藉由**推廣藍染這項傳統手作技藝，團結**

蔡秀惠不斷參觀臺灣各項藍染特展以精進技術。

社區意識，自創品牌，喚醒隱而不見的歷史，唯獨曾是藍染重鎮的頭城，對於這段遺失的文化，仍無具體的思考、辯證與傳承。是在這樣的擔憂之中，懷擁真摯，全心全力投入其中——2022 年 9 月至 12 月，蔡秀惠接受頭城鎮福成社區發展協會的邀請，開設 30 堂藍染課程，帶領在地民眾重新認識藍染。

> 藉由喚醒藍染的記憶，展開鄉鎮與土地一連串在地產業的迢遙歷史追尋。

溯回消隱的技藝，增添新時代的潮流，新舊交集，共匯時光。為了精進技術，蔡秀惠不斷參觀臺灣各項藍染特展，由同時代的作品，反照觀看自身不足，同時在網路的分享影片中，學習不同的藍染技術。嘗試，再嘗試，除了鞏固基本技術，更開始細膩構思，頭城所能孕育的獨特藍染風格。提煉藍泥，或用菁粉添水，備好染布，再以棉線、橡皮筋、瓶蓋、彈珠、竹筷子和冰棒木棍等基本器物輔助，賦予各式圖樣。那是我們未能深入理解的藍染，是創作靈感，是構圖設計，是衣褲百物的外顯形象，以深淺的藍，或留白，或浸潤，或複染，精細含括土地中的自然萬物。

1

2　3

1 蔡秀惠在社區裡教授藍染技藝。

2 在宜蘭的山區裡，山藍也生長繁茂。（圖片提供：蔡秀惠）

3 藍染的運用極廣，從布料到帆布袋都可利用。

　　喚醒失去的記憶，從來就不是一件容易的事，正是因為不易，才值得去做，春來江水綠如藍，我們可能都忘了，藍色是最溫暖的顏色。

‧‧‧

Profile

頭城早年是宜蘭的藍染重鎮，然隨著化學染興起，傳統藍染逐漸式微，近年來復古風潮興起，這項傳統技藝又漸漸受到重視。蔡秀惠是倡導傳統藍染的工藝復興者，目前有在福成社區活動中心授課，傳承技藝，並曾在蘭陽博物館展覽作品。

用手機掃描QR code，
深入認識頭城職人生

▲收聽訪談

Tsai Siou-huei is an accomplished tailor in Toucheng who offers a wide range of services—from fashion design to clothing/trouser repair. She began her career as a wedding dressmaker and soon gained recognition in her community for her exceptional skills. But she didn't stop there. Instead,

Tsai Siou-huei:
Tailor, Indigo Dyer & Owner of **Siou-huei Tailor Studio**

she continued to hone her skills by learning indigo dyeing, a technique of dyeing cloth with natural dyes extracted from plants.

In recent years, she joined the Yilan Natural Dyeing Development Association (established in 2016) and participated in dyeing technique workshops. Her works were exhibited in the "Out of the BLUE— An Exhibition on Yilan Indigo Dyeing" a few years ago. Now, with years of hard work and experience, she has become a master and advocate of indigo dyeing, striving to promote this art craft and introduce the history of the indigo dyeing industry in Toucheng to even more people around here.

The heyday of indigo dyeing in Taiwan can be traced back to the 1880s, during the Qing Dynasty, when natural indigo dyes from Taiwan were in great demand—ranking third among the island's exported products. However, with the successful development of synthetic indigo by the German company Bayer AG, producing natural dyes through plant cultivation became inefficient and costly. As a result, the indigo dyeing industry saw a sharp decline in the early 20th century, and by the 1940s, the cultivation of indigo dye plants had ceased altogether.

Toucheng, a town that once boasted a thriving indigo dyeing industry, suffered a severe decline. There used to be around 28 households who were engaged in related work and many dyeing workshops on Heping Street. But today, you can only find one surviving structure on Heping Street—the remains of the former dyeing workshop, Yuan He Cheng Store.

Reviving a nearly-forgotten past and making it known to others is never an easy task, but it is a worthwhile endeavor. Hopefully, in the future, more people will come to know about indigo dyeing and fall in love with the warm and comforting hue it creates.

鏤彩織雲霞

——拼布手藝與謝籃傳承・賴淑真

德安堂中藥房傳至賴淑真的先生，已是第三代。

夫家祖父薛金在原本是一位種田農民，農閒時期編起謝籃，以手工製作器皿貼補家用。上山採竹，巧遇老中醫，兩人相談甚歡，老中醫便開始教授基本的藥草知識。薛金在運用藥理知識幫助鎮民，予以抓藥養病，端視情況免費推拿，久而久之傳開名聲，開設中藥行，鎮民都知曉「謝籃仔阿在伯的中藥房」，傳承至今，成為開蘭路上的德安堂中藥房。

開設中藥房期間，薛金在同樣編織謝籃，過程不假他手。山林砍竹，運送下山。開剖，削去兩邊硬皮，竹篾循序交織綑紮，細火烘烤竹片使其彎折，爾後細密編織。編後抹上塗料，再飾以花草釉漆、祥瑞鮮果與吉祥話。做工嚴謹，程序繁複，成品扎實耐用，一個謝籃平均足足要花一個星期才能完成。坊間稱讚：「謝籃在的謝籃會當（可以）貯（裝）水。」如今，宜蘭地區能以細膩工法編製謝籃，以及彩繪花紋的師傅近乎失傳。

何謂謝籃？早期謝籃出現於訂婚、結婚、迎娶等場合，每個場合均有其禮俗規範。以出嫁女兒而言，謝籃是給女兒裝載嫁妝的容器，擺放龍眼、木屐、紙扇等，以及出嫁可能會用到的器物，蘊含祝

福，希望女兒嫁到夫家能夠不愁吃穿；而在宜蘭當地，則有特殊的「閃冬」習俗。此外，謝籃亦會在神明生日、長輩生日、嫁娶等重要場合出現，盛裝符合各個節慶的吉祥物品，大多重複使用，不隨禮品送出。

　　薛金在十分重視編製謝籃的技藝，對於工藝成品的要求相當高，不願文化的傳承被隨意糟蹋；同時因年事已高，沒有合適與願意承接的人，頭城竹

賴淑真發揮女紅精神，將縫補織錦的技藝運用於不同生活物品。

製謝籃的技藝就此失傳。作為一位拼布藝術家，賴淑真深諳謝籃的文化意義，結合巧思，運用自身擅長的手藝，**藉由「裁縫」與「拼布」，製作布製謝籃，賦予古物全新樣貌，期望將謝籃與德安堂中藥房的故事延續下去。**

> 謝籃用於嫁娶、神明或長輩壽辰等場合，盛裝吉祥物品，大多重複使用。

如今，為了延續阿公的助人精神，中藥房時常給予民眾各種幫助，包含賒帳、抓藥解惑等，意圖將善意繼續傳播下去。此外，中藥房亦予創新，製作防蚊香包，以及藉由參與頭城老街藝術季相關活動，積極推廣助人為善的理念。

近年來，賴淑真主要從事拼布藝術創作。剪碎布料，依據畫面深淺焦距，以不同色系的棉布、蠟染布相互拼貼縫合。仔細拿捏布料特性，思考距離，完整呈現近、中、遠景的光影層次，巧手拼縫的作品，內容包含頭城車站、龜山朝日、搶孤等在地風情，每一件作品的完成無不曠日廢時。此外，發揮女紅精神，將縫補織錦的技藝運用於不同生活物品，例如福龜、抱枕、手提布包、防蚊香包、全身衣飾等，試圖將所謂的拼布藝術，點點滴滴編織於生活。

另一方面，賴淑真重新思索自身的宜蘭噶瑪蘭

| 1 | 2 | 3 |

1 賴淑真的拼布作品。
2 賴淑真發揮布藝專長，以布製作謝籃來傳承。
3 薛金在的傳統謝籃技藝，現已失傳。

後裔身分，次次進行思辨、定位與再次認同。臺灣早期的原住民，都有被汙名化的現象，作為現今語言文化幾乎消弭的宜蘭噶瑪蘭平埔族，亦在漢族強勢移墾的歷史情境中，或舉家南遷，或隱身漢族。2017 年，開始發想、設計、製作精緻的噶瑪蘭族服飾，全新改良，希望**透過族群服飾的重新展現，再次找回自我的認同**；同時，闡述這段幾乎湮滅的歷史，提醒整個社會，必須對於多元族群保有尊重。

　　輾轉往復，針織雲霞，一位創作者的使命，其實不單囿於技藝的表達形式。拼布藝術家賴淑真所做的努力，正如知名動畫《詩人的生涯》，母親傾注血肉生命才得以編織的殷紅毛衣，帶著疼惜、祝福以及對於家鄉的恆久深情，溫暖覆蓋未來的子嗣。

Profile

頭城德安堂為薛金在因緣際會創立的中藥店，同時製作謝藍販售，至今中藥房傳承至第四代，已逾百年，謝藍則從竹編轉為布製，由賴淑真將謝藍代表的文化意義，傳遞下去。

用手機掃描QR code，深入認識頭城職日生

▲ 收聽訪談　　▲ 臉書粉專

Lai Shu-zhen and her husband are the third-generation inheritors of De An Tang Chinese Medicine Shop, a famous Chinese medicine shop on Kailan Road, Toucheng Township, Yilan County. The medicine shop was founded by Lai's husband's grandfather, Xue Jin-zai, who used to be a farmer who made

Lai Shu-zhen:
Patchwork Artist & Co-operator of De An Tang Chinese Medicine Shop

hand-woven bamboo wedding baskets (containers for carrying dowry in the past) and hand-crafted utensils during his free time to supplement the family income. One day, while Xue was gathering bamboo in the mountains, he met an old Chinese medicine doctor. They hit it off right away and had a great time chatting. The old doctor began teaching Xue basic knowledge about medicinal herbs. Xue used the medicinal knowledge he had gained to help townspeople with their illnesses and gradually developed a reputation. Eventually, he opened a Chinese medicine store, which has now been passed down through the generations up to the present day.

Xue continued to make bamboo wedding baskets after the medicine shop was opened. He carefully attended to every detail of the intricate process without the assistance of others. It would take him about a week to finish one basket, but the finished product would be of high quality and highly durable, woven together with beautiful colorful patterns. The community lauded Xue for his masterful craftsmanship, proclaiming that his baskets were so well-made that they could use them to store water. Nowadays, there are scarcely any artisans left in Yilan who can make bamboo wedding baskets with such master craftsmanship.

Despite not having the bamboo-weaving skill, Lai, guided by a commitment to preserve the traditional wedding basket practice, made the best use of her patchwork expertise and innovatively incorporated patchwork art into wedding-basket making. In fact, Lai devotes much of her time to creating patchwork art in recent years. When creating her art pieces, she meticulously considers the unique properties of each fabric, carefully plans the layout of the final image, and artfully cuts, collages, and sews together fabrics of different colors and textures (e.g. cotton and wax print fabric) to bring her vision to life. Much time and effort is spent on each piece. With her exceptional craftsmanship and skillful use of light and shadow, she presents famous local scenes such as the Toucheng Station, Guishan Island at dawn, and Qianggu Festival, with an impressive spatial layout that features varying levels of depth and distance.

With each pull of her needle and thread, Lai weaves beautiful images, hoping to not only create captivating artworks but also contribute to the preservation and promotion of the traditional wedding-basket custom of her hometown, for the benefit of future generations. To this end, she's willing to do her utmost, which echoes the devotion of the mother in the celebrated Japanese animation "The Poet's Life (1974)," who stitches a warm sweater for her son at the cost of her own "blood and flesh."

情感的顏色肌理

藝術工藝

—用畫筆記錄家鄉・黃興芳

線條，輪廓，顏色，鉛筆作畫的沙沙聲從家鄉方向悠然響起。

黃興芳，又名鉛筆馬丁，1962 年出生宜蘭，長於頭城十三行。著有繪本《記得那海的味道》、《繪憶・頭城 - 馬丁的童年》、《繪夢烏石》。20 幾歲離開家鄉，前往臺北謀職。擇定方向，以動畫為業，曾任動畫製作、檢查、原畫、構圖、構圖指導、人員培訓、腳本分鏡、造型設計、場景設計、企劃、主管等職，40 多歲已從基礎工作晉升動畫導演。離鄉已有半甲子，歸返只是偶爾，直到父母相繼過世，才赫然發現生命產生巨大的幽暗裂隙。

沉思面對，亦是暫時凝止，故鄉的召喚從靜默中浮現。黃興芳表示，父母離世，無疑是自己必須面對的生命關卡，心中知曉，勢必尋找一些方式，讓起伏迴旋的情感有所平緩。

不知何去的失路，於是自然而然拿起熟悉的鉛筆，進行記錄。作畫當下，是緩慢的釋然，是安靜的沉澱，是延緩的行拍，遠處的自己跨越時光遠渡千里，彷彿最

終，尋回最初的自己，踏上腦海深處的家鄉。再度歸返，一切滄海桑田，人事已有極大落差，有些記憶遭遇遮蔽，無法經由再次探查而清晰憶起，必得藉由一幅一幅畫作復現過往。黃興芳表示，返鄉的理由相當私我，自己只是一位普通的頭城囡仔，畫作只是個人的情感表達，曾經懷疑這樣的思索與畫作，或許不值得分享。

「用自己的筆，記錄自己的家鄉，透過這個方式，把自己的情感表達出來，跟家鄉產生連結。」

最初使用鉛筆作畫，來自直覺。鉛筆是作畫根本，服裝、建築與場佈等設計工作，時常以鉛筆作為初始構圖。筆尖觸碰紙張，或疊合，或遊走，或

生活與藝術是一體的，他思考、生活、領受……緩慢挖掘，然後表達於畫紙上。

凝止，正如一位游子重新回返故鄉展開踏尋，不知下一刻線條將左彎右拐，不知移動路線將蜇入巷弄或步履山海，不知浮現的輪廓將描摹現今或撫觸過往。是以，紙筆浮現的一切，同時疊合自我情感、地景特徵與集體的文化記憶，畫中有海岸、山巒、田野、建築、廟宇、老街、烏石港、搶孤，以及每一位生活其中的人。

經由畫作，以及文字紀錄，不知不覺帶著自己走得如此遙遠。黃興芳表示，生活與藝術是一體的，面對故鄉，必須用最自然的方式緩慢挖掘，這樣的過程，能讓自己愈趨安靜，感受精神的真正平靜。畫作不再是純粹的地景復刻，而是創作者對於故鄉的真摯投射，只有生活其中，才得以領受。這樣的過程，不僅能夠與跟當地產生連結，亦能透過鄉親的認同與共鳴，真正找到回家的感覺。

這當然是一種尋根。頻繁回望頭城的黃興芳，年年參與「金魚厝邊」從 2015 年開始舉辦的「頭城老街文化藝術季」相關活動，除了以繪畫記錄頭城的往昔變化，更在和平街和中庸街等街巷牆壁，留下迷人彩繪，彷彿意圖藉由個人的藝術力量，重新

> 藉由作畫，與家鄉產生連結，透過鄉親的認同與共鳴，真正找到回家的感覺。

1

2

3

1 走入社區，記錄生活。
2 在街巷牆壁留下迷人彩繪。
3 以自己的畫作導覽頭城，更見細膩觀察。

喚醒眾人對於在地的抒情想像。

　　任何創作，都是積累、轉變與思索的過程。黃興芳不曾停止思考，深入生活，次次展開不同形式的創作，如鉛筆、壓克力顏料與文字紀錄等。創作之餘，進行分享，走入社區，步入校園，將內在的色彩、自省與經歷，轉譯成另一種具有啟發性的顏色肌理——那是透澈發現自己，完全打開，彷彿將生命視為一幅最最明朗的畫。

...

Profile

原本從事動畫工作，返鄉畫下心中的頭城，開始新的創作之路。他說自己習慣用鉛筆畫畫，喜歡線條的隨意轉變，就像自在散步的不經意。每一幅圖都充滿鮮活的生命力。

用手機掃描QR code，深入認識頭城職日生

▲收聽訪談　　▲臉書粉專

Huang Xing-fang (Martin) is a pencil artist with a number of illustration works to his name, including "Recalling the Smell of the Sea," "My Childhood Memories in Toucheng: Depicted in Illustrations," and "Wushi Harbor in Illustrations:

Huang Xing-fang:
Pencil Artist Depicting the **Hometown in Illustrations**

A Nostalgic Journey to My Hometown." Born in 1962, he grew up in Shihsanhang, Toucheng Township, Yilan County, and left to pursue a career in animation in Taipei in his 20s. He started from humble beginnings and became an animation director in his 40s—only occasionally returning to his home in Toucheng. However, as he worked towards his career dreams, he was dealt with a devastating blow of the successive deaths of his parents, leading him to reassess what was truly important in his life.

Lost and bewildered, he picked up a pencil and started to draw some illustrations. Drawing brought him inner peace, and as he continued to record life in his illustrations, memories of his hometown came flooding back, prompting him to return. As he set foot again in his hometown, he realized that it had undergone immense changes. People and things were very different from before, and many scenes from his memories were gone forever. Moved by this realization, he decided to return home and use illustrations as a medium to preserve his childhood and hometown memories.

"I want to use my pencil to capture the beauty and charm of my hometown and express my feelings towards it, rebuilding the connection with my hometown."

Unconsciously, he has been using illustrations, complemented by some words, to express his feelings and record his life for many years. According to him, life and art are inseparable, and for an artist who centers his work around his hometown, it takes time and patience to truly discover and capture its beauty. In his personal experience, the process gives him a sense of tranquility and inner peace.

For him, depicting one's hometown in illustrations is not simply about replicating the beauty of a landscape, but also about communicating the artist's innermost feelings about the place where they come from. This can only be achieved by actually living in the place. After returning to his hometown, Huang has re-established the bond with his community, gained recognition from fellow townspeople, and made his works resonate more with them, truly experiencing the joy of coming home.

在地產業

老有所養

—— 以添大之名跨入居家無障礙環境・林士傑

　　頭城和平街，矗立許多時代遺留的老建築，其中，一家以製作無障礙環境器具的公司座落其中。這裡曾是宜蘭第四屆縣長林才添（1903 ～ 1989）的故居，經由孫輩林士傑的重新規劃、打造與整修，已然迥然不同——簡易的招牌，樸拙的外貌，有種不刻意彰顯的調性。

　　老屋充滿宜室宜家的簇新感。二樓寬敞明亮，擺設眼前的，是祖父一生戮力服務的解說年表，是祖父畢生受贈且由書法名家康灩泉所題匾額，是添大興業產業變遷的示意圖，是往昔家業製造的一顆顆珠圓玉潤的礙子（高壓電桿上的絕緣體）。作為名流後代，林士傑散發儒雅的文人氣質，一方面承接庭訓，一方面**以其生命經驗，轉譯無障礙友善空間的重要性。**

　　1938 年，林才添在宜蘭頭城創立「蘭陽窯業株式會社」，專門出產紅磚瓦片。1950 年，易名「添大興業股份有限公司」，轉型為高壓電瓷礙子製作工廠；當時全臺灣只有兩家礙子工廠，添大為其一，鼎盛時期曾有一百多位員工，養活一百多個家庭。2014 年，林士傑為了陪伴罹癌的父親，給予支持，辭掉上海工作返回臺灣。2016 年，沿襲家族企業之名獨自創業。

　　「我是半路出家，一切都靠自學。」林士傑就讀臺大政治系公共行政組，後來曾經從事輔具販售、輪椅業務等工作，以添大興業之名，跨入居家無障礙環境改善，其實源於照護父親的親身經驗。林士傑整修老宅，一方面揣度銀髮輪椅族的需求，考量移動的方便性、居家的安全性；另一方面，則是為了成立創業辦公室。檢視居家環境，拓寬浴室門，加裝扶手方便起身，浴室地板鋪以抿石子防止跌倒，高低階梯裝設斜坡板方便移動。初期的設計擘劃，實際施工，以及後續展望，這一切都**來自照護父親而積累的經驗**。

林士傑決定轉型為居家無障礙改善服務，將古厝當成辦公室。

回憶過往家業，林士傑表示，無論祖父林才添或父親林義剛，都具有一種難能可貴的職人精神。印象最為深刻的，就是全體員工下班之後，父親仍然待在工廠，研究配方，使用儀器做實驗——父親全神貫注的神情，深深烙印腦海。林世傑秉持父輩精神，將其意志，輾轉活化於不同產業，不論是工序的細節、品質的把握、移動路線的規劃等，均無遺漏，意欲將服務做到最好。

> 添大興業隨時代轉型，從紅磚瓦片、瓷礙子製作廠，現跨入無障礙環境改善。

這並非是單純的商業行為，更是一件具有意義的事情。

林士傑希望自己的經驗，能夠成為一顆種子。我們所面對的是——人口老化、高齡海嘯的未來，必須要先照顧好家中長者，才能讓年輕人無後顧之憂。**預防勝於治療，投身於此，不倦衛教，積極倡議居家無障礙概念，**包含考量長者出入，防範跌倒，揣度輪椅移動路線等；乃至對於公共空間發出建言，如何庇護傷殘進出，馬路與人行道如何消弭高低落差等。更進一步放遠眼光，建議政府支持民間設立關懷據點、日照中心與安養院，穩健發展長照產業。

林士傑一心諭示，其實是我們共同的未來。

1 牆上有許多祖父受贈的牌匾，是傳家之寶。
2 以往添大興業以生產礙子為主。
3 從照顧父親的經驗中，發現輪椅使用者的需求。（圖片提供：添大興業）

前方還有很長很長的路，還能來回跋涉，直到走不動——那時，我們將會坐在輪椅上，雙手施力，繼續奔馳如同煙花燦爛的年少。

■■■

Profile

「添大興業」由已故前宜蘭縣長林才添創立，早年生產磚瓦，後來製作「礙子」，近年因電線地下化而式微。其孫林士傑 105 年返鄉創業，承繼品牌，轉型為居家無障礙環境服務。

用手機掃描QR code，深入認識頭城職日生

▲收聽訪談　　▲臉書粉專

Tien Ta Development Co., LTD., now headed by Lin Shi-jie, is a company in Toucheng that provides home accessibility planning and construction services. As a family-owned business, this company did not have its origin in this particular line of business.

Lin Shi-jie:
Present-Day Owner of
Tien Ta Development Co., LTD

It was first founded in 1938 by Lin Cai-tian under the name of Lanyang Ceramic Corporation as a red-brick and tile manufacturer. In 1950, the company changed its name to Tien Ta Development Co., Ltd. and shifted its focus to high-voltage ceramic insulator production, becoming one of the only two high-voltage ceramic insulator manufacturers in Taiwan at the time. In its heyday, the company had more than 100 employees, supporting more than 100 families. In 2016, the company was taken over and transformed into a home-accessibility company by Lin Shi-jie, Lin Cai-tian's grandson, who quit his job in Shanghai and returned to Taiwan to take care of his cancer-stricken father in 2014.

"I didn't receive formal education in this field, so I

had to learn everything through self-education." In college, Lin Shi-jie studied political science (public administration) at National Taiwan University. Before taking over the family business, he worked as a salesperson selling assistive devices and wheelchairs. But he wasn't aware of the importance of home accessibility until he returned to his hometown Toucheng to take care of his father. To provide better care for his father, he renovated the family's old house for easier wheelchair access, making it safer and easier for the elderly to move around. Throughout the process, he accumulated considerable experience in planning and carrying out home improvement projects and assessing their effectiveness, which has later become the cornerstone for him to set up a home-accessibility company.

While devoting himself to home accessibility improvement, Lin Shi-jie has also been actively advocating for the concept of barrier-free homes, believing that prevention is better than a cure. He stressed the importance of accounting for the needs of the elderly, creating a home environment that can protect the elderly from falling and allow the wheelchair to move around easily. He also proposed various suggestions for improving accessibility in public spaces, including how to better assist the disabled in entering and exiting buildings and to eliminate level differences between roads and sidewalks.

Lin Shi-jie dreams of a future where society values environmental friendliness for the elderly more, hoping that his experiences can serve as a tiny seed to bring it into reality. He noted that, since the aging population trend is likely to persist in the future, it is important to ensure that the home environment is safe and accessible for the elderly so that the working-age population can focus on work without having to worry about their elderly family members at home.

舌尖的記憶之旅
在地產業
——吳記古早味鳳薯酥‧吳肇民與蕭鳳真

食物本身，擁有多重的複雜性與意義性。初始用來溫飽人類，而後則用來祭祀祖先、部落共享以及宗教互惠，因此，食物自然被賦予進食以外的禮節儀式。

祭祀前後，透過相同目的，獲得天地君王庇佑，同時藉由相同味道相承食譜，確認各個社群對於舌尖記憶牽動的認同、界定與價值，進而完成神鬼與天地的共享，彷彿由此，再次拉近彼此的親密關係。是以，**食物與其牽涉的餚饌宴席，通常都與文化脈絡、政治經濟、宗教秩序形成緊密的互動。**

在地美食，往往是重要的地方性人文景觀，凸顯區域文化，以及區域本身孕育的獨特個別性（Individuality），尤其是特色小吃。頭城老街的「吳記古早味鳳薯酥」的堅持、傳承與創新，在在顯示此種難能可貴的人文精神。傳承已至第四代，現由第三代吳肇民與蕭鳳真主事，第四代的兄弟吳承峰和吳承翰則在假日協力幫忙。

非謀生事業，非觀光工廠，非經由設計師精心設計符合大眾想像的伴手禮風，

四代傳承共同製作食物的過程,不但拉近家族之間的距離,更與文化產生緊密連結。

　　吳記古早味鳳薯酥的產品,兀自**散發無可取代的迷人手作性格**。或許該說,這些產品的世代承接重新誕生,基本上,是為家族與整個小鎮,留下無可取代的歷史記憶。

　　第二代吳增壽,1924 年生,從南洋當兵返臺,向岳父周元(第一代創始人)學習庶民小吃的製作方式,當時種類繁多,有米篩目、番薯酥、花生糖、花生粉糖、麻仔糖、牛皮糖(盹龜糖)、芋粿、蘿蔔糕、粉條等。吳增壽努力創新,研發配方,使所有糖類甜點都清爽不黏牙。

　　現今,產品種類稍減,同時因應季節而有區分。夏有米篩目、粉條,冬有鳳薯酥(地瓜酥)、花生粉

糖和豆干，一年四季都產花生糖。農曆二月初二土地公生日，曾經替頭城老街南門土地公廟製作花生糖龜，鑼鼓歡慶，食予甜甜，向土地公年來的護衛表呈謝意。每年農曆六月初六，則會自主舉辦米篩目祭，取其諺語「六月六食米篩目，予恁趁錢淹腳目」。2018年，蕭鳳真自發推動米篩目傳承，原先單純為了回饋鄰里，而後受到地方仕紳鼎力支持，投注經費，最終無償烹飪米篩目供鄉親享用。

> 食物不僅是食物，還與文化、政經、宗教緊緊連結，更是小鎮的歷史記憶。

　　除了**藉由食物傳達情感，同時主動加入各種社區活動**，包含吳肇民家族於元宵、中秋等節日，擔任不同宗教慶典主持；頭城媳婦蕭鳳真投入頭城老街導覽、花生糖製作講解、蘭博志工和宜蘭社大志工；夫妻倆共同參與宜蘭縣福氣家族公益協會等。種種活動，不求回報，自主付出，這一切都讓我們見識到，何謂真正的民間力量。

　　「吃」的驅動與指向，足以作為一種關乎原初的身分認同（Identity），那是對自

	2
1	
	3

1 夏日間，米篩目冰深受歡迎。

2 農曆六月初六，舉辦米篩目祭，無償烹飪米篩目供鄉親享用。（圖片提供：吳記古早味鳳薯酥）

3 以手工將米漿過篩至熱水中，急速冷卻後，添加到冰和糖水，就是夏天受歡迎的品項。

我、社群與文化主體的再次認定。吃什麼，不吃什麼，如何吃，如何不吃，這一切舌尖腸胃之事，深深牽引每一個人的過去、現在與未來——那可能是記憶的醒轉，是鄉愁的繚繞，更是我們對於所在之地，最最忠誠的歸依。

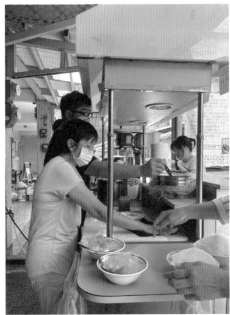

■ ■ ■

Profile

吳記古早味鳳薯酥有百年歷史，已傳承四代，2019年榮獲頭城經典小吃美食，夏天製作手工米篩目，添加簡單剉冰、糖水，來一碗讓你暑氣全消；冬天製作豆干、花生粉糖及傳統的古早味蕃薯酥。

用手機掃描QR code，深入認識頭城職日生

▲收聽訪談

▲臉書粉專

Local foods, especially snacks, often serve as an important representation of local culture. A prime example of this in Toucheng, Yilan, is the Wu Ji Traditional Snack Shop, located on

Wu Jhao-min & Siao Fong-jhen:
Current Owners of
Wu Ji Traditional Snack Shop

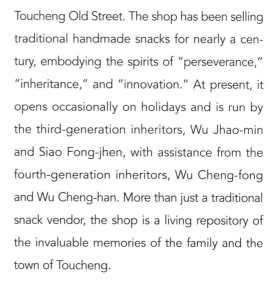

Toucheng Old Street. The shop has been selling traditional handmade snacks for nearly a century, embodying the spirits of "perseverance," "inheritance," and "innovation." At present, it opens occasionally on holidays and is run by the third-generation inheritors, Wu Jhao-min and Siao Fong-jhen, with assistance from the fourth-generation inheritors, Wu Cheng-fong and Wu Cheng-han. More than just a traditional snack vendor, the shop is a living repository of the invaluable memories of the family and the town of Toucheng.

The founder of the shop was Jhou Yuan, whose son-in-law, Wu Zeng-shou, learned how to make everyday snacks for ordinary people from him and became the second-generation successor. In the past, the shop sold a wide range of snack products, including rice sieve noodles, sweet potato pastries, peanut candy, sesame candy, taro cake, turnip cake, starch noodles, etc. Nowadays, the variety of snacks has slightly decreased, and different items are sold in different seasons—rice sieve noodles and starch noodles in summer, sweet potato pastries, taro cake, and dried tofu in winter, and non-sticky peanut candy all year round.

In addition to selling traditional snacks, the shop has always been actively engaged in local events. For example, on the second day of the second lunar month, which marks the Earth God's birthday, the shop prepares peanut candy in the shape of tortoises as an offering to the Earth God, whose temple sits at the south gate of Toucheng Old Street, as a way to thank him for protecting the region throughout the year; on the sixth day of the sixth lunar month, in response to an old Taiwanese saying which roughly means that eating rice sieve noodles on this day can bring prosperity, the shop hosts the Rice Sieve Festival to wish everyone prosperity and good fortune.

The shop also seeks ways to give back to the community. For instance, in 2018, one of the shop owners, Siao Fong-jhen, launched a program to promote the preservation and transmission of the rice sieve noodle making skills, and later, thanks to strong support and funding from local residents, she was able to offer rice sieve noodles to community members for free.

Treat yourself to a local snack offered by Wu Ji Traditional Snack Shop! You might be amazed by how delicious it is, be reminded of your past or your attachment to your hometown, or even be inspired to reimagine the present and future in a brand-new way.

金石錚錚時日暖

——為鐵工業注入設計美學·徐宏達

頭城老街，漢人入蘭早期開墾的鮮明見證，象徵代代相承的歷史。從慶元宮廟埕往南，步行數十公尺，左側即見一間向內延展、住家改建的在地傳產——「和發」鐵工廠。

和發商店，頭城第一家鐵工廠，技術精湛，聲名遠播，現已傳承至第三代。沒有招搖招牌，沒有眩目指示，如同廠內兩側各式機具設備、精工器材和金屬備料，具有內斂穩重的性格。鐵漢低頭，背脊駝彎，手持焊槍、鐵鎚和夾鉗等沉重工具，時而謹慎量測，時而精準搥打，眼神與金屬原料在接觸時刻，射放令人顫動的熠熠火光。

徐宏達，1980年生，畢業於復興美工，曾經從事水電，現為鐵工廠老闆，是土生土長在地青壯。其另一身分，是頭城東嶽廟興安堂會長，支持地方宗教，積極推動神將文化。古銅膚色，剽悍神情，留著一頭即肩染色長髮，頗有日本視覺系藝人模樣。

祖父原居金瓜石，從事鐵製鉛片等加工製作，而後遷移頭城，傳產技藝遂代代相傳。店內主要製作鐵門、鐵窗、鐵皮屋和鐵捲門，更提供其他客製化商品服務，曾經製作鐵窗花、金屬福州門、重型機車專用斜坡、浪板吊架、白鐵捕鰻

弓形架等。早期的鐵製產業，鐵匠擁有彈性的設計空間，對於鐵窗花的需求較大；現今的鐵工市場，大多僅只考量機能、實用和費用，功能與藝術不再並進，製作鐵窗花的顧客相當少，可能一百間只餘一、兩間。即便如此，徐宏達仍然兀自堅持，無論何種業務託付，成品務必堅固耐用。

　　徐宏達表示，從小耳濡目染，熟悉金屬零組件，再加上熟能生巧，自認從事鐵工並非特別困難；接管家業之後，直截面對產業，心中卻顯得五味雜陳。技術可以傳承、延續與開展，絕非囿限親族，可惜鐵工業的流動率過高，人力斷層嚴重，如今和發鐵工廠

徐宏達的外型頗有日本視覺系藝人模樣。

除了自己，還有一位師傅和一位學徒。大多時候，鐵工廠只有一人，校長兼損鐘，得瞻前顧後，得向同行借調人力，得婉拒超出負荷的龐大工程。探究原因，其實跟鐵工所被定義的社經位階，以及承擔的風險有關。藍領粗工，向來不受重視，得捎重物，得忍受日曬雨淋，長期下來不僅可能傷損筋骨，一不小心更有可能發生墜落等嚴重職災。

人力斷層使鐵藝面臨失傳，民間宗教的鐵器與迷人的鐵花窗是否會成追憶？

「鐵工業爬得比別人高，搬得比別人重，賺得卻沒有比別人多。」口氣帶著無奈。

技藝一旦失傳，也就難以尋回。對於未來，徐宏達希望能夠朝向鐵製品精緻化的路線，為鐵工業注入設計美學，讓平民的日常生活擁有金屬質地般的沉穩；另一方面，徐宏達勉力呼籲，希望這個看似衰落的夕陽傳產，能夠獲得相對應的薪資，能夠確保鐵匠權益，並且受到社會廣泛尊重。

此外，徐宏達亦在思考，自身的專業如何結合在地宗教，曾經特別製作鐵製燭臺、廟宇柵欄、神轎頂架、陣頭移動推臺、舞龍舞獅的龍頭等。**鐵工傳產與民間宗教，兩者範疇看似相異，卻在徐宏達**

| 1 | 3 |
| 2 | |

1 在高溫危險中作業的鐵匠，無論是專業與薪資都需要被重視。

2 以鐵打造神將道具、廟宇文化用品是未來的發展方向。

3 將鐵工往鐵藝方向提升，是徐宏達的心願之一。

身上，有了不相牴觸的完善統整。

　　金石錚錚，一個一個蹲踞爬高的身影，一次一次彎曲伸直的骨幹，一條一條扭折形塑的鐵條，彼此碰觸，高溫之中以煙花招呼，以灼光言談，以火舌擁抱。我們似乎不曾發現生活的所在，鐵器製作的歷程，存在隱而不現的強悍技藝，以及恆常陪伴的溫柔記憶。

■ ■ ■

Profile

和發商店是頭城第一家鐵工廠，專營鐵門、鐵窗、鐵皮屋、鐵卷門等客製化商品，現已傳承至第三代徐宏達。他希望鐵製品能夠朝向精緻化路線，為鐵工業注入設計美學，同時結合宮廟文化。

用手機掃描QR code，深入認識頭城職日生

▲ 收聽訪談

▲ 臉書粉專

He-Fa Ironworks, widely known for its superior craftsmanship, is the first blacksmith shop in Toucheng, which has now been passed down to the third generation. Plain in its exterior with no

Hsu Hung-da:
Skilled Blacksmith & Owner
of He-Fa Ironworks

eye-catching signs or indicators, the blacksmith shop brings a sense of calmness and trustworthiness to its visitors—much like the impression conveyed by the various machinery, precision instruments, and metal materials inside the shop. As you walk in, you see a blacksmith with his head down and back hunched over working intently on ironwork. With the aid of heavy tools like welding guns, hammers, and pliers, he meticulously measures and skillfully shapes the metal through precise hammering. As sparks fly in every direction, his eyes shine with sparkling radiance.

The blacksmith is Hsu Hung-da, born in 1980 in Toucheng, Yilan. Before taking over the family business, he went to Fu-Hsin Trade & Arts School and worked as a plumber and an electrician after

graduation. With bronze skin, shoulder-length dyed hair, and a tough look, he bears a striking resemblance to a Japanese visual artist.

He-Fa Ironworks was founded by Hsu's grandfather, who initially resided in Jinguashi (a former mining town in Ruifang District, New Taipei City) and worked in the iron and lead processing industry before moving to Toucheng Township, Yilan County, and passed down his skills to his descendants. Today, the shop's primary focus is on manufacturing ironware such as iron doors, iron windows, iron-sheet houses, and roll-up doors and providing customized products or services.

The iron industry has now become a seemingly sunset industry. Acutely aware of the importance of preserving traditional craftsmanship as once a skill is lost, it is extremely difficult to recover, Hsu has been dedicating himself to reviving this declining industry. He strives to incorporate innovative design and aesthetic elements into ironwork to create more delicate iron products and attract more people back to using ironware. He also urges society to protect blacksmiths more, giving them more respect and better pay, as they are the ones who possess this invaluable craftsmanship.

Iron products are common items in our daily lives, but they are created through an extremely arduous process. It often requires the blacksmith to repeatedly squat down, climb up, bend over, and straighten his torso as he forges the iron through repetitive hammering, heating, and annealing. The final products, crafted through hours of labor, display exquisite craftsmanship and can often accompany us for a significant portion of our lives. It would be a great pity if this craftsmanship is lost one day.

心中永遠的孩子——

催生元宵孩子龍‧徐錫南

文化教育

孩子龍，專屬孩子的熱鬧慶典，經由在地力量的匯聚，進而形塑獨特的文化。成人暫時退出舞臺，禪讓位階，讓孩子成為主角，倘佯於無憂無慮的童年，同時，讓我們重新遇見自己心中，那一位仍然尚未長大的幼童，回到純粹、快樂與每一個人最初的模樣。

徐錫南，成長於頭城老街，孩童時期喜好於慶元宮玩耍。臺北工專（現為臺北科技大學）電機科畢業，離鄉遷居臺北，曾在臺灣水泥與幸福水泥工作，現已退休，擔任頭城文化發展協會監事。

耆老緩緩述說孩子龍的歷史起源——

頭城早期元宵有「炸龍」習俗，南、北門均有舞龍，兩區民風不同，調性歧異，南門強悍為武龍，北門風雅為文龍。最初炸龍由成人主導，光裸上身，脖頸綁一條毛巾勇猛踏入炮陣。民國 50 年元宵，開蘭路與菜市場展開激烈炸龍，火花四射。早期民眾相信元宵炸龍，象徵祥瑞，不僅能夠興旺店家生意，參與者還能身強體健驅邪避凶，甚至認為炮陣火花能夠消毒，抑制瘟疫。鞭炮四起，車拚炸龍，南北兩條舞龍意外起火，最後祝融吞噬一無所剩。

爾後兩年，元宵無龍可舞，僅有礁溪聯華電池廠退伍軍人以敦親睦鄰之名舞龍，約二十分鐘便匆

匆離去，孩子無不失望。民國 53 年，頭城囡仔不甘
寂寞，在慶元宮廟埕自製舞龍，用竹畚箕做龍頭，
用草繩做身體，用高麗菜竹簍做嘴巴、耳朵和尾巴，
用竹籬笆做支撐桿，用舊報紙做龍珠，最後拼拼湊
湊自得其樂做成一條吉祥玩具龍，並從廟埕舞至開
蘭路與民豐路——**孩子龍正式誕生**。鄉親熱切支
持，給予材料經費，希望活動能夠長遠續辦。隔年，
為了避免浪費資源，選用堅固鐵絲，並從「畚箕龍」
進化為「鐵龍」。

　　徐錫南表示，孩子龍的誕生，來自孩子的童
貞，來自鄉親對於孩子的關愛，藉此活動，具體展
現一種自發性的地方文化力量。

退休後回到頭城，開始製
作舞龍，重建對於故鄉的
情感。

可惜的是，孩子龍的活動還是中斷數十年。直到 2015 年，徐錫南等耆老回鄉，舉辦同學會，重新認識頭城的人文地景風土文化，才發現自己對於家鄉並不熟稔，孩童製作舞龍歡慶元宵的記憶，再次返回腦海。源此契機，開始製作舞龍，重建對於故鄉的情感。2016 年，推廣相關活動，由成人製作舞龍骨架，再由小孩彩繪。此後年年舉辦，擴大規模，包含元宵前由孩子自行製作舞龍，以及元宵當日的古早童玩遊戲、燈籠製作、藝文表演、人文故事分享、猜謎、書法揮毫、孩子龍團隊踩街等。頭城鎮各區域小學，將舞龍製作列入課程，社區、協會與地方團體踴躍參與，宜蘭國際童玩節甚至將此活動納入表演。

> 吉祥孩子龍的誕生，來自孩子們的童貞，也來自鄉親對於孩子的關愛。

這是記憶的再次尋回，亦是節日蘊藏的力量。**如今，每一個頭城社區，都有一條舞龍**，藉由慶典，讓孩子參與民俗活動，腳踏實地認識家鄉。所有的遠方都由近處出發，所有的行動都由當下實踐，對於地方文化的認同，頭城文化發展協會努力匯聚多方力量，徐錫南亦不曾止步——那是鄉土對於人們的祝福，是大人對於孩子的關愛，是孩子對於家鄉

	1	
2	3	4
		5

1 孩子龍以竹竿、竹簍製作而成。

2 3 頭城早期元宵有「炸龍」習俗，民間認為可趨吉避凶。

4 重組孩子龍的動機是對孩子的關愛。（圖片提供：徐錫南）

5 如今每個頭城社區，都有一條舞龍，讓孩子參與民俗活動。

的熱情，點點滴滴，風風火火，排成邁向前方的堅強陣列。

　　元宵佳節，得提燈籠，得吃湯圓，還得至頭城看孩子舞龍。

■ ■ ■

Profile

　　徐錫南等耆老重組「孩子龍團隊」，與頭城文化發展
協會在 2016 年共同推動「龍歸故里孩子龍慶元宵」
文化活動，讓消失數十年的「孩子龍」，再度在元宵
節重現頭城街上。

用手機掃描QR code，深入認識頭城職日生

▲收聽訪談　　▲臉書粉專

Xu Xi-nan spent his childhood on Toucheng Old Street and later went to Taipei to continue his studies. After graduating from the Provincial Taipei Institute of Technology (now known as

Xu Xi-nan:
Founder of **the Children's Dragon Dance Tradition**

the National Taipei University of Technology), Xu moved to Taipei and worked for Taiwan Cement Corporation and Lucky Cement Corporation. Now, he is the supervisor of the Yilan County Toucheng Cultural Development Association.

In the early days of Toucheng, there used to be a custom during Lantern Festival known as "Dragon Bombing," where groups of shirtless adult dragon dance performers, with a towel tied around their necks, danced for fortune amongst the firecrackers. According to Xu, there were two types of dragons. The one from the South Gate was imbued with a martial spirit, while the one from the North Gate emanated a kind of refined literary temperament. The Dragon Bombing event used to be seen as auspicious since people back then believed that it could bring prosperity to the local community and fortune and good health to the participants, and that firecrackers

had a "sterilizing" effect that could help prevent the outbreaks of plagues. However, in 1961, when the dragons met at Kailan Road and the nearby traditional market, fires accidentally broke out because too many firecrackers were set off at the same time. Many people were injured and the dragons were burned.

In 1962 and 1963, the Dragon Bombing event was halted, leaving local children rather disappointed. In 1964, Xu (who was still a child then) and other kids came up with the idea of making their own dragon. They collected materials near the Qingyuan Temple on Toucheng Old Street and successfully created a dragon, using the bamboo dustpan for the dragon's head, straw rope for the dragon's body, cabbage basket for the dragon's mouth, ears, and tail, bamboo hedge for the support pole, and old newspaper for the dragon ball. Upon finishing, they self-contentedly performed dragon dance from the temple to Kailan and Minfeng Road, receiving great support and encouragement along the way. That's how the tradition of children making dragons and performing a dragon dance during the Lantern Festival first came into being in Toucheng.

The tradition was later interrupted for decades. Fortunately, it has been revived in recent years—thanks to the great efforts made by Xu Xi-nan, the Yilan County Toucheng Cultural Development Association, and many others. Today, each community in Toucheng has a dragon, and there are many projects encouraging children to participate in dragon-making and dragon dance activities—with adult assistance provided when needed. The revival of the tradition is invaluable as it perpetuates a unique local tradition and offers an opportunity for children to learn more about and bond with their hometown and a chance for adults to show their love and care to the younger generation. It's a tradition full of blessings, a tradition that helps strengthen the emotional connection between the land and its inhabitants, and a tradition that holds a special place in the memories of many.

常處樂，興於仁——巷弄裡老屋內的長照站長・陳柏瑞

公眾環境

建築的存在意義，在於情感，以及人與空間共同展開的抒情生活。

傳統建築不僅需要妥善保留，更重要的，在於如何鞏固既有基礎，予以翻新，完成內外的改造、再生與重新定位。傳統街區老街古宅的保存，透過修繕，輕巧活化，**其核心價值絕非僅止商業考量，而須以傳統建築的在地集體記憶、人文價值與共有財產概念，進行內部思考。**頭城老街中的「新長興樹記」，藉由空間的重構，醫療系統的注入，讓人群復返，日日踏穿門檻，完成老屋新居醫療長照的成功典範。

時光之流再次以其日常樣貌，汩汩流動，銀髮的時日煎熬，將能贖回悠遠的歲月靜好。

陳柏瑞，1964 年生，現為宜蘭市開蘭安心診所院長，主治家庭醫學，擔任全家福社區醫療群計畫執行中心負責人、宜蘭縣松齡協會理事長、宜蘭縣愛胰協會常務監事等職。頭城曾是漢人入蘭第一城，石港春帆，一片繁景，隨著經濟重心南移羅東（林業砍伐），曾是頭城最大的南北雜貨批發新長興樹記，生意開始走了下坡。陳柏瑞從小棲居古厝，直到小學一年級，父親在喚醒堂附近開設明和興雜貨店，才舉家搬遷。子孫陸續離鄉，老屋年久失修就此荒廢。

陳柏瑞認為長照必須有獨特的在地性，他開始探索適合宜蘭的長照模式。

　　建築前身為「長興行」，原為一式三間，現今留存「新長興樹記」與相互比鄰的「老紅長興」，皆屬昭和時期建築。風格外西內中：建材為鋼筋混凝土及洗石子，支撐柱則以洗石子搭配紅磚；屋內採傳統中國式木構造。狹長型街屋，共分兩進，前為商業空間，後為自用住宅。2007 年 3 月 8 日，新長興樹記公告為縣定古蹟，予以研究、保護與修復。此外，老宅古蹟亦作為重要據點，2021 年成立 C 級醫事巷弄長照站，舊址再次出現自在走動的人潮，接納白叟，迎來長者，予以妥善照護。

　　這無疑是一種精神式的回返，以及再度出發。曾經看顧過陳柏瑞的長者，已然白髮皤皤；如今，學有所成的陳柏瑞回到出發長成之地，斥資改建，投注感情，盡自己的力量為鄉親序大（長輩）服務。

　　「凡事須以仁德作為基礎。」這是陳柏瑞為人處世重要理念，這樣的精神，恰恰啟蒙於新長興樹記的門上對聯：「常處樂，興於仁。」

陳柏瑞帶領自己的醫療團隊，以其專業，進駐頭城。那是整合的過程，從器官導向的疾病醫治行為，延伸至以照護為導向的身心長照服務，醫療服務只是其中一個面向，**如何結合醫療與照護才是重點**。茲因於此，層層深探：如何縮短老年殘障期？醫療的極限與界線？如何結合不同的專業領域？人的本質為何？老人家想要的究竟是什麼？

> 藉由空間的重構，醫療系統的注入，完成老屋新居醫療長照的成功典範。

「並非追求經濟規模，而是想要探索適合宜蘭的長照模式。」陳柏瑞特別指出，長年觀察之中，高齡長照有一明顯特徵，那就是需要個別化照護，無法概括論定。每一位老人都有各自的想法、故事、歷史脈絡，憑仗自身過去的背景、經驗、家庭作為對比，由此找到自我價值。是以，完善的長照，除了公部門資源和社會團隊的力量之外，更必須具有獨特的「在地性」思考，一種專屬頭城的模式。陳柏瑞更提出，高齡長照可由長者之間的互助，大大減輕社會負擔。

醫療團隊跨入長照，不是一件容易之事，然而陳柏瑞的思考不僅於此，試圖再以良善的空間，**創造一處長者日常活動相互照看的所在**。老宅新屋，

	1
2	3

1 2 老人家在此從事各種活動，在社區中變老是最理想的狀態。

3 老宅新屋，曾經繁華落盡的新長興樹記，又重現人潮。

曾經繁華落盡的新長興樹記，再次送往迎來接納人潮，再次往復走踏交流情感，這裡明亮、整齊、溫暖，充滿過去和現在的人情記憶，還有一雙一雙手，穩穩牽引我們走向未來。

在此生根，於是無懼落葉。

■ ■ ■

Profile

開蘭安心診所佇立於蘭陽平原 20 年，期間不斷地思考與翻轉醫療的理念與責任，後帶領自己的醫療團隊，以其專業，進駐頭城，設立「新長興樹記 - 巷弄長照站」，透過長照的照顧，讓長輩活得更健康自在。

用手機掃描QR code，深入認識頭城職日生

▲ 臉書粉專

A building is not merely a physical structure, but a symbol of nostalgic history that continues to evolve. While it is important to preserve traditional buildings, it is even more crucial

Chen Po-juei:
Driving Force behind Yilan's Long-Term Care Services

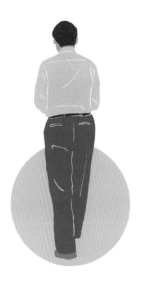

to properly renovate and repurpose them for modern use with a thoughtful approach. "Xin Chang Xing Shu Ji" (a townhouse on Toucheng Old Street) is a successful example of architectural renovation and repurposing. Through redesigning and the introduction of medical systems, it now serves as a long-term care station.

"Xin Chang Xing Shu Ji" was originally part of the three-building complex known as "Chang Xing Store." Today, only two buildings, namely "Xin Chang Xing Shu Ji" and the adjacent "Lao Hong Chang Xing," remain from the original complex—both were constructed in Japan's Showa era, boasting an elegant exterior. On March 8, 2007, "Xin Chang Xing Shu

Ji" was designated as a county-level historic site, and in 2021, a long-term care station (Level C) was set up there.

The driving force behind the establishment of this long-term care station, as well as other long-term care facilities in Yilan, such as the Charmstays Daycare Center established in December 2022, is Dr. Chen Po-juei, director of the Kaillan Group Practice Clinic. Born in 1964, Dr. Chen specializes in family medicine and upholds the belief that "benevolence and morality should be the basis for everything we do." He derived this belief from the couplet he saw on the front door of "Xin Chang Xing Shu Ji," which generally means: Long-lasting happiness and prosperity come from benevolence.

"A good long-term care service should prioritize developing a model that is most suitable for the local community, rather than pursuing its size and scale." With years of observation under his belt, Dr. Chen highlighted that elderly individuals require personalized care and that having support and resources from both the public sector and community organizations, as well as developing a model that is tailored to local conditions, is necessary and crucial. He also noted that if long-term care programs can foster mutual assistance among seniors, the burden of the elderly on society can be significantly reduced.

With such a vision in mind, Dr. Chen and his medical team have put in great efforts towards this goal. They work tirelessly to create bright, tidy, warm, and caring long-term care spaces where the elderly can assist each other in their daily activities, receive attentive care from medical professionals, and live future days happily and fearlessly right here in Yilan.

公眾環境

巷仔口的味道──

叭噗與社區服務・黃志安

叭噗就是我的名字。

黃志安，1965 年生，「阿宗芋冰城」第二代，九歲即削第一顆芋頭。第一代為黃錫宗，人稱芋冰宗，採用臺灣在地芋頭，用搖搖冰原理自學自製叭噗，純手工，非奶製品，不含任何化學添加劑。

黃錫宗共生四子，為求養家，除了自製薄利多銷的芋頭叭噗，凌晨更兼差殺豬，冬日擺攤販售紅豆餅，長久下來積勞成疾，54 歲即不幸病逝。黃錫宗原先反對子女接續家業，認為製冰操勞，無所出頭；三子黃志安從復興工商專科（後為蘭陽技術學院，現已停招）畢業之後，不願手藝就此失傳，果決承接，大膽創新。1973 年，黃錫宗正式登記為勝美冷凍庫，做叭噗與冰棒的自產批發；1975 年，更名阿宗芋冰城；2004 年，黃志安在青雲路三段開設實體店面。

「咱若有才調（本事），手骨就愛伸出去。」父親的話，黃志安不曾忘卻。

如今，阿宗芋冰城可謂頭城遠近馳名、不可錯過的甜點。不管是在地人或外來客，叭噗早已成為集體的味覺記憶，召喚往事，並以鮮甜的味道、綿密的口感，帶來滿足微笑。事業的成功，

讓黃志安留存餘裕，思考如何妥善運用自己的力量，回饋所得。2015 年，接下「城東社區發展協會」理事長 (現為常務監事)，服務至今，其理念為取之社會，用之社會，想為社區好好盡一份心力。「欲做就做予好，莫予 (被) 人嫌──」

　　所謂**在地認同，必須透過地方的社群發展，傳達出一種共同參與、協力合作的公共性。**黃志安釐清思緒，審度自己究竟能夠做些什麼：投入經費，檢視協會年度計畫，予以補強、豐富與創新，除了例行性的自強聯誼活動、年度會員大會之外，更加強老仙角志工隊社區服務內容。此外，年年籌辦大型活動，包含頭城話中秋、重陽敬老晚會等。

黃志安從賣叭噗的小攤位到成功的店面，並成為積極投入社區發展的實踐者。

2019 年成立「三老故事房」（位於慶元宮後方中庸街），其名三老，是為老人、老事與老物。巷弄間的三合院經過改建，具有多元功能，現為協會主要活動中心和社區關懷據點。空間足可契闊談讌，提供銀髮共餐；同時成立家政班，清明做草仔粿，端午做肉粽，冬至做圓仔湯等。黃志安表示，舉辦這些活動，都是為了讓老人家能夠走出家門。

在地認同透過地方社群發展，才能傳達出共同參與、協力合作的公共性。

三老故事房的核心價值在於保存、珍視與傳承，藉由舉辦相關活動，讓年輕一代能夠知曉地方的人文歷史，保留時代精神。以「頭城耆老話中秋」為例，活動包含攻炮臺、龜、擲筊比賽、蒙眼打鼓、福宴等，結合地方特色小吃，一方面凝聚社群意識，一方面重現頭城早年中秋盛況，一方面推廣蘭陽特殊的食物風味。

「這個地方我從來沒有離開過，我是真正的在地頭城人。」從賣叭噗的小攤位，到成功的店面，再到積極投入社區發展的實踐者，黃志安一路走來，不改初心，沉穩踏實，以自己可能的力量，竭力為生活所在，注入源源不絕的資源。一球小小的叭噗，緩慢吞吐，終而成為最為慷慨的祝福。

1 「三老故事房」經過改建，具有多元功能。
2 成立志工隊為社區服務。
3 頭城文化相關活動，黃志安都熱心參與。

■■■

<u>Profile</u>

三老故事房是老街巷弄間的三合院改建而成，三老
是指老人、老事與老物，這裡具有多元功能，現為協
會主要活動中心和社區關懷據點，也是頭城鎮城東
社區第二休閒中心。

用手機掃描QR code，深入認識頭城職日生

▲收聽訪談

▲阿宗芋冰城

Huang Zhi-an is the second-generation successor of A-Zong Ice Treat Shop, a traditional ice treat shop in Yilan best known for its "Ba Pu ice (taro flavor)." This ice treat looks like ice cream but is different in that it is a non-dairy product. Its name

Huang Zhi-an:
Current Owner of
A-Zong Ice Treat Shop

comes from the way it was sold in the early days—street vendors would use a special air horn that made the "ba-pu" sound to attract customers.

Huang Zhi-an learned how to peel the taro root at age 9 from his father, Huang Xi-zong, the founder of A-Zong Ice Treat Shop, who taught himself how to make this handmade, non-dairy, chemical-free ice treat made of locally-farmed taro through the shaking method. "If you're capable, you should be responsible and do what you can!" Huang Zhi-an never forgot his father's words.

Today, A-Zong Ice Treat Shop is famous far and wide, and the "Ba Pu ice" they sell has become a must-try treat in Toucheng for both locals and tourists. Characterized by its delightful sweetness and creamy texture, the ice treat brings a profound sense of pleasure to anyone who has had the opportunity to taste it. Over time, it became a nostalgic taste that is cherished and reminisced by many.

After achieving success in his career, Huang Zhi-an started to think about what he could do for the community. In 2019, he converted the traditional courtyard house on Zhongyong Street (behind the Qingyuan Temple) into a "Story House" to present stories that revolve around the elderly, traditional practices, and historical objects in Toucheng. The space is now used by the Chengdong Community Development Association as an important activity center and a community care site, where the elderly can socialize, dine together, and participate in a variety of courses or activities, such as making herbal rice cake (or "caozaiguo") on Tomb Sweeping Day, rice dumplings (or "zongzi") on Dragon Boat Festival, and glutinous rice balls (or "tangyuan") on the winter solstice. These activities, as Huang Zhi-an noted, are meant to encourage the elderly to step outside their homes and engage in social and cultural events.

In addition to providing a gathering place for the elderly, the "Story House" also serves as a space for cultural heritage preservation and transmission. Events are held to help the younger generation gain knowledge and appreciation of the local culture and history, preserving the spirit of times past.

"I have never left Toucheng and I am a true native of this place." Once a vendor selling ice treats at a stall, Huang Zhi-an is now an ice treat shop owner and has been actively involved in community development activities. He maintains a down-to-earth attitude and remains committed to his original cause, making every effort to give back to the community.

流觴曲水墨留香

文化教育

—— 傳承蘭陽書法之美・康潤之

「蘭陽康氏」，宜蘭頭城最富盛名的書法世家，現已傳承至第四代康潤之。

日治時代，康潤之的曾祖父康灩泉（1908-1985），榮獲日本國際書法比賽特賞殊榮，被譽為「蘭陽第一筆」；祖父康介珪（1928-1996），將書法藝術應用於匾額，使作品長遠留存，被稱為「蘭陽第一匾」；父親康懷（1959～），為人低調簡樸，韜光養晦，延續家風，歷年獲得國、內外重要美術獎項，曾舉辦多次書法展覽；**康潤之（1986～）承繼父親創設的「康懷工作坊」**，除了續存既有的書法藝術、匾額製作之外，更運用大學多媒體設計系習得的影像美學、數位影音、互動媒體等新時代技術概念，進行創新，包含經營臉書專頁、設計文字 Logo、藝術共創等，賦予書法繼往開來之全新意義。

康家字體，以清代「趙之謙的魏碑」作為書寫基底，爾後揮毫隸書、行書、草書、篆書等，無不留存其神。字體渾厚夯實，氣度沉穩恢宏，如隱見蒼茫天地，酣暢墨水無不彰顯堅定神韻。

康潤之表示，琴棋書畫自古以來專屬文人雅士，對於平民百姓而言，可謂奢侈。由於家境並不殷實，須得努力賺取早晚餐飯，祖父一輩曾經下定決心，不再花錢購買毛筆宣紙，書法文風可能由此

斷代。幸而，學校老師識得康懷的書寫天賦，強力
勸勉，鼎力舉能，最終獲得康灩泉允諾。康潤之從
小耳濡目染，浸潤家教，父輩並不強迫以筆墨為職，
不要求承繼家業，而將書法視為修身養性的法則。

　　書法為日常，而非謀生賺錢之道。

　　康潤之也有自己的叛逆時期，坦承國、高中不
學無術，上了大學，開始有所轉變。上學期間半工

「蘭陽康氏」為宜蘭頭城最
富盛名的書法世家，現已
傳承至第四代康潤之。

半讀，貼補家用，退了伍，回到家鄉陪伴逐漸老邁的父親，繼續從事藍領工作，甚至曾經參與雪山隧道和下水道等工程。康潤之表示，小時候比較喜歡畫畫，長大之後，心境日趨平穩，退伍返鄉重新開始書寫書法，漸次察覺其中奧秘。

> 書法為**修身養性**的法則，使其回到日常，**躬身力行**，尋常且恬淡，謹慎且敬重。

「寫書法能夠感覺身體內部的氣流，調整自己的氣息。情緒會影響字，奇妙的是，時常寫完之後，氣流就通了。」書寫的主要目的，不是為了比賽，不是為了傳承，不是為了博取名聲，而是類似日常作息，時間到就寫。

康潤之清晰思辨，坦率自陳，書法像是即將被淘汰的夕陽產業。現代生活之中，撰寫書法幾乎無法維生，**為了生存**，必須跟異業互動、**結合與共創**。「我盡可能用傳統書法去做創作，如同在規則邊緣，不去超過。」對於康潤之而言，自創書寫字體不是一件難事，重點在於，如何在資本主義當代社會，同時實踐生活的飽足與藝術的追尋，是以沉潛求變，方寸收放，賦予創作彈性。

那是延續，承接與開創，頭城老街文化藝術季至今已臻七屆，第一、二屆由康懷參與，第三屆起

1

2

3

1 揮筆間能夠感覺身體內部的氣流，調整自己的氣息。

2 3 康潤之從傳統中創新，並以不同的字體表現（圖片提供：康潤之）

交棒康潤之。而在書法子弟康潤之身上，具體呈現一種在地與國際的文化連結，不僅在「金魚厝邊」長期協助之下，舉辦「靜心—書法」文化體驗工作坊，更借助書法藝術，與不同的國際創作者合作交流。

康潤之不受盛名所累，重新思索家風庭訓的現代意義，讓書法回到日常，躬身力行，尋常且恬淡，謹慎且敬重，蘭陽康氏彷彿因而替所有從事藝術的族裔，樹立氣定神閒無所動搖的表率。「盡可能用生活去做引導，用環境去影響，過程中用篤行的方式呈現。」康潤之磨墨展紙，手執毛筆，眼神凝定面色清明，徐徐吸氣，緩緩吐氣，黑墨白紙之中，穩健展開一趟河清海晏的旅程。

白日飛歌聲不止，流觴曲水墨留香，生活如字，書寫者將以各自的字跡浩瀚展開。

■■■

Profile

「康懷工作坊」為蘭陽康氏第三代康懷創設，擅長書法與雕刻藝術創作，作品獲得國內外諸多獎項肯定。目前由第四代康潤之承繼，重新思索家風庭訓的現代意義，讓書法回到日常。

用手機掃描QR code，深入認識頭城職日生

▲收聽訪談

▲臉書粉專

Kang Run-zhi is a famous calligrapher from the Kang family, a renowned calligraphy family in Toucheng, Yilan. His great-grandfather, Kang Yan-quan (1908-1985) won the first prize in the national calligraphy competition held in Japan

Kang Run-zhi:
Heir of a Distinguished Calligraphy Family in Yilan

during the Japanese colonial era, earning him the title of "Best Calligrapher in Yilan." His grandfather Kang Jie-gui (1928-1996) applied the art of calligraphy to plaques to better preserve calligraphy works for future generations, attaining the title of "Best Plaque Calligrapher in Yilan." His father Kang Huai (1959-), though low-key, has continued the family legacy. He has won numerous art awards at home and abroad over the years and held multiple calligraphy exhibitions. In 1986, he founded a calligraphy workshop called Kang Huai Calligraphy Workshop.

Kang Run-zhi decided to follow in their footsteps and became a calligrapher. In addition to preserving the traditional art of calligraphy and creating calligraphy plaques, he applied what he had learned in college as a multimedia design student— including the concepts and use of visual aesthetics, digital multimedia, inter- active media, etc.—to calligraphy. By incorporating calligraphy into the logo design, practicing art co-creation, and using Facebook fan pages for promo- tion, he breathed new life into the art of calligraphy, imbuing it with a new and contemporary meaning.

"When I write calligraphy, I feel and regulate the Qi in my body. Qi and emo- tion changes may be reflected in our calligraphy writing, and one amazing thing about writing calligraphy is that it helps process negative feelings and promote the flow of Qi; I often feel much better after finishing my writing." For Kang Run-zhi, writing calligraphy does not have much external purpose; it's not for submitting to any competition, or for gaining fame, or even for cultural transmission. He writes calligraphy because it has become part of his daily rou- tine. At a certain point in time in the day, he just naturally starts to write.

Despite achieving great fame and success, he remains faithful to his family's commitment to it, dedicating himself to preserving the traditional art of cal- ligraphy while endeavoring to endow it with modern meaning. He cultivates himself through calligraphy writing, becoming a composed, meticulous, and respected person.

"Art should be closely linked to life and the world around us and be put into practice," said Kang Run-zhi in a calm, reassuring manner. He, along with the Kang family in Toucheng, seems to demonstrate the demeanor and qualities that an artist should possess, setting a good example for future artists to follow.

公眾環境

不僅二三事

——頭城在地網路社群—頭城二三事版主

這是一個網路的當代，一個眾聲喧嘩的年代，更是一個藉由社群媒體廣泛交流的新型世代，從口述、隨筆、照片，乃至正式的公文、通知、文獻等，資訊都以各自的觀點同時聚集。訊息潮湧流動，功能時效不長，短則以時，長則以日，隨即被下一刻的大小新聞淹沒。這是後現代的特徵，拼貼、消融、交互衍生、遠近混搭，個體的發聲匯流成集體的複音。

「頭城二三事」，即是一個現代在地社群的運作楷模。

2013 年 9 月，土生土長的板主騎乘腳踏車，行於頭城街巷，腦海浮現念頭，若有一個公開的平臺能夠分享鎮內消息，那麼必定能對家鄉有一正向助益。

當時，雪隧開通七年，頭城已有不同的社群進駐，陸續開設店面。版主指出，許多店家開幕，因為鎮上缺乏良善平臺，無法分享資訊，最後無人關注，只能默默倒閉，相當可惜。從此起心動念，開始記錄，並且公開發表。最初開設臉書粉絲團，後來為了讓更多人參與，滿足各式需求，轉

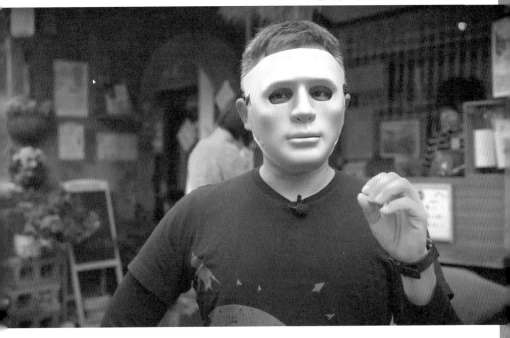

為 Line 社群，2022 年則正式推出「小烏龜 App」。

頭城的在地定居或長期居留的人口相當多元，包含在地人、衝浪客、宜蘭縣立人文國民中小學家長、島內移民和青年返鄉等，設立網路社群，是為了打造一個橫向的溝通平臺，以其立即性、功能性與公開性等特徵，發揮推波助瀾的功能。**「小烏龜 App」，專門針對頭城人提供服務，**內有各式版面，包含閒聊版、二手交易版、公共事務版、房屋出租版、求職版、店家好康版等，個人或店家均可主動貼文，若有需求亦可分類查詢，公開回覆。

網路的公共空間，亦可連結生活，產生實質活動。曾經以臉書粉絲團串聯一百個店家，策畫頭城

以社群連結生活，持續打造一個不斷向眾人開放的公共討論空間。

文創園區市集，網路空間則用來介紹店家、近期活動與鎮內動態。板主表示，透過網路社群自身的活潑力量，致使平臺成為一相互增添、彼此挹注的有機體，不斷豐盈充實，從新店開幕、理念溝通、藝文活動分享，乃至容納不同的政策規劃等，各種聲音自由出入，意見紛呈，各自評析，最終將可能達到「正向的螺旋」。

在人口多元的頭城，網路社群不但是居民們即時溝通的平台，更是種生活服務。

當然，這只是資訊的中介，而非公共事務主要的建言管道，重要的是，由此平臺加強民眾與社區的雙向關係。除了提供公共的討論空間，板主更期待「頭城二三事」能夠成為時代的見證，例如透過影像呈現圖書館改建、老屋翻修、頭城車站前後轉變等，數位存檔留駐網路，進而成為珍貴的記憶公共財。

社群網路的介入，絕對不僅虛幻，即刻資訊互通有無，共匯聲音將能見證一時一地多元看法，留存的文字影像，正是具體映現集體歷史。言雖二三，心卻齊一，「頭城二三事」板主，正以新世代的思考，有條不紊的行動，從網路連結生活，持續打造一個不斷向眾人開放的公共討論空間。

| 1 | |
| 2 | 3 |

1 透過頭城二三事，讓頭城生活更豐富。

2 拿出手機拍照分享是日常，他常在街上收集新資訊然後分享。

3 小烏龜 APP 功能更多，有租屋、二手交易與各種活動。

■ ■ ■

Profile

「頭城二三事」臉書粉專與 LINE「頭城二三事互助社群」，不但連結了頭城小鎮與居民，更是外地人想知道最新訊息的最佳方式，想收到最新好吃好玩與人事物訊息，一定不能錯過，趕緊訂閱起來。

用手機掃描QR code，深入認識頭城職日生

▲收聽訪談　　　▲臉書粉專

"Little Things in Toucheng," originally a Facebook fan page and later also a LINE OpenChat room, is a great modern example of creating local information-sharing platforms and promoting community development initiatives.

Creator of
Little Things in Toucheng and
Little Turtle

The Facebook fan page "Little Things in Toucheng" was established in September 2013 by a native of Toucheng, who, when riding a bike, came up with the idea of setting up a public platform for local information sharing. Having observed that, though the opening of the Hsuehshan Tunnel in 2006 had since prompted many new stores to open in Toucheng, many of them closed down shortly after opening due to a lack of information dissemination, he was convinced that creating such a platform would be of great benefit to the community.

He was right. After he started to record local information and post it online, he received many positive responses. Later, to engage more people and fulfill more needs of the community, he created a LINE OpenChat room and then launched an app called "Little Turtle" in 2022—specially designed for people of Toucheng. There are many sections in the app, including Chat Section, Second-Hand Item Trading Section, Public Affairs Section, House Rental Section, Job Search Section, Shop Special Offers Section, etc. Both individuals and stores can post information, and if there is a need, they can search by category and respond publicly.

The person behind all this aimed to leverage the dynamic power of social media to create spaces where community members could share information (e.g. information about new store openings and arts/cultural events), exchange different perspectives, and discuss various issues (e.g. policy issues) freely. He expected to see more people get involved and a broader range of voices and opinions be heard and expressed, creating an upward-spiral dynamic.

With a modern way of thinking, he has created amazing interactive spaces for community members in Toucheng, setting a great example of how to connect the internet, daily life, and the local community in a meaningful and sustainable way.

公眾環境

一封一封寫給故鄉的情書
——李榮春文學的傳頌者・李士儀

他們的這一夜是很平常的，並沒有什麼特別的地方。他們的這一夜也是很平靜的，但在這種平靜的表面下，卻有一種甚深至情的激動。那就是一種對於永恆的無可如何的悵惘。　李榮春，《鄉愁》

頭城鎮中庸街，藏隱一條文學巷，以在地文人歷年作品作為主軸，巷道逼仄，卻自有遼闊的精神視野，其中，我們必須記得一個名字：李榮春。

一位被臺灣文壇忽略的文學家，一位在歷史夾縫中進行創作的失語者，一位力圖用故事建構記憶的收藏者，一位對於故土懷有至情的囡仔，一位慣習沉默的書寫者——所被忘卻，亦須記起，才得以知曉過去，原來之後的我們，都是由時代傷痛所生下的孩子。

小說家李榮春（1914～1994）出生頭城，排行老四。1938 年，曾受臺灣總督府徵召，以臺灣農業義勇團身分，至中國開闢軍用農場，植疏種菜，供應日本皇軍伙食。而後往返移動於日本、臺灣與大陸。1946 **年，自中國返臺，立志餘生專注於書寫。**《祖國與同胞》八十萬字，是生前唯一出版的作品。書寫完畢，隨即藏諸書櫃，累積三百萬餘字，直屆傷逝，才由家族整理遺稿，先是交付李潼評看，後由學者彭瑞金編纂，並由晨星出版社於 2002 年出

李榮春姪孫女李士儀擔負起後繼者的使命。

版全集。著作具有強烈自傳性，或描述中國經歷，或書寫頭城家鄉，留下的故事，無疑是時代賦予的饒衍餽贈。

　　書中是日常的閩南生活，是特殊的宗教慶典，是家族的交際往來，是無法復返的在地紀錄，是母親，更是一生熱切懷抱的故土。孤隱者一生奉獻，近乎宗教式的真誠獻身，無視物質生活，透過書寫的極限可能，辯證文學的價值，探究存在的意義。略有艱澀的文字，難

以擴編的生活情節，無非是那一整個喑啞時代，禁錮於身的明顯特徵。書寫，成為唯一大事。

> 李榮春餘生立志專注於書寫。留下的故事，無疑是時代賦予的饒衍餽贈。

李士儀，1979 年生，是李榮春姪孫女。李士儀表示，記憶之中，伯公沉默寡言，衣褲潦草不修邊幅，卻是一位樸實誠懇相當溫暖的人，面對人群始終面帶微笑。往昔，每個禮拜二禮拜五，小說家都會搭乘公車至羅東，同家族成員吃一頓飯，再坐著公車返回頭城獨居寫作。

「規工佇寫，也毋知佇寫啥。」李士儀的阿公曾說。

這不僅只是家族之事，更是歷史之事，**李士儀帶著後繼者的使命，努力推廣李榮春文學**。2022 年夏，主動凝聚一群地方文史學者，成立「李榮春文學推廣協會」。我們必須坦承，文學在現代社會之中逐漸式微，不易推廣，然而正是因為艱難，才值得前行——有些永恆價值，只有文學才能完善給予。基金會舉辦多起活動，包含文學走讀、出版《李榮春全集》電子書、《李榮春文學通訊》刊物、文學紀錄片推廣、文學與音樂跨越合作、文學市集等；接下來的計畫，還包含出版選集與繪本，舉辦文藝沙

1 在李榮春於和平老街留影。(圖片提供：李士儀)
2 李榮春文學館中展示其著作與手稿。
3 地方文史學者共同創立李榮春文學推廣協會。

龍，意欲連結東北文史力量，使李榮春文學推廣協會成為宜蘭重要的文學據點。活動紛呈，緩步實踐，俾使文學滲入日常，匯聚一股溫暖且恆常的力量。

　　從一位文學的內向隱者，到一個文學社群的外展擴編，我們所見，是文學家對於故鄉的熱愛，是文學的後繼者對於土地的敬重。真正的文學，始終會被留存下來，而我們都應該成為其中的一分子。那麼要如何開始呢？**或許展讀作品，或許前來文學巷與李榮春文學館，或許慢慢步行於小說家筆下永恆的頭城故土。**

■■■

Profile

李榮春文學館位於頭城開蘭東路 4 號，原為頭城國小舊校長日式宿舍，陳列作家李榮春影像手稿、寫作地景及為文學理想堅持不輟的一生。目前由頭城鎮公所管理，同時具備頭城老街導覽諮詢功能。

用手機掃描QR code，深入認識頭城職日生

▲收聽訪談　　　▲臉書粉專

Lee Rong-chun (1914-1994), born in Toucheng, Yilan, was the fourth child in his family. In 1938, he was recruited by the Taiwan Governor-General's Office to be a member of the Taiwan Agricultural Militia.

Lee Shih-yi :
Promoter of Lee Rong-chun's Literature

He went to mainland China to build military farms, grow vegetables, and prepare food for Japanese soldiers, and also traveled back and forth between Japan, Taiwan, and mainland China multiple times. In 1946, he returned from mainland China and devoted the rest of his life to writing. He hid his works, totaling more than 3 million words, in the bookshelf after completing them. Only one of his works, "Homeland and Compatriots," which had a word count of 800,000, was published during his lifetime. The rest of his works were only discovered by his family after he passed away.

His family sorted his manuscripts and showed them to Li Tong, a famous Taiwanese writer, for review. The manuscripts were later edited by Peng Rui-jin, a renowned scholar in Taiwan literature, and published by Morningstar, Inc. in 2002. His works, encompassing his experiences in mainland China and stories that took place in his hometown Toucheng, feature strong auto-biographical elements and give us a glimpse of what life was like in the past.

Lee Shih-yi, born in 1979, is Lee Rong-chun's grandniece. She remembers her granduncle as a warm, quiet man who always greeted people with a smile, despite not caring much about how he dressed. He used to take a bus to Luodong, Yilan, every Tuesday and Friday to have a family reunion dinner and then take a bus back to his home in Toucheng, Yilan, where he lived and wrote alone.

For Lee Shih-yi, promoting Lee Rong-chun's literature works is not simply a family matter; it is of great historical significance. Therefore, in the summer of 2022, she approached a group of local scholars in literature and history. Together, they set up the Lee Rong-chun Literature Association.

Works of literary value deserve to be preserved, and we should all join the ranks of literature promotion and preservation. How can we begin? Well, perhaps we can begin by reading more, visiting literature museums, or set-ting foot in the hometowns of our beloved writers. Lee Rong-chun Literature Museum and Toucheng are excellent choices for such visitors.

船過水留痕：繁極一時的水運盛況

帶路人
講故事

莊漢川
出身頭城望族，
跟著他的導覽走
讀頭城，有非常
豐富的收穫。

沒有一般老街的喧囂，頭城老街記載宜蘭河的變遷，靜靜地沉積在和平街上。

剛到頭城，站在人車來往的台二線上，細細體會這一條曾經為重要的河道，列為蘭陽八景「石港春帆」的風貌。

頭城老街就是和平街，兩端各有南北門土地公廟守護；中間是慶元宮，也是一間歷史悠久的媽祖廟，短短的 500 公尺，敘述著百年「開蘭第一城」河道的潮起潮落。

宜蘭為扇形沖積平原，平原上多丘陵地，加上多雨、颱風因素，造成宜蘭地區河道變化非常大，從對外貿易的烏石港時代（1796 ～ 1878），到宜蘭西北貨物進出的頭圍港時代（1863 ～ 1924）；無論是運送鎮內作物如大青、茶葉的內港（現址南門福德祠），或是運送對外的大眾物資如稻米、甘蔗的外港頭圍港（現址盧纘祥宅的史雲湖），因應而生的十三行、鳳梨市（現址已

不可考）都顯示航運是當時頭城很重要的運輸方式，直至 1924 年東部縱貫鐵路開通、頭圍港淤塞，結束了一百多年來水運的繁華時代。

　　走在沿著河道建立的老街，仔細觀察遺留下來的牆面，依照防水強度各有不同面貌：下層用石頭及三合土推砌而成、中層為磚牆，最上層用土角夯實，用祖先的智慧層層堆疊，也讓路過的人們細細品味。（口述／莊漢川，文字／楊宇伶）

■■■

1. 莊漢川正在解說這段採紅磚與拱柱的百年街屋。2. 慶元宮位於老街中段。3. 看似池塘但曾經是頭圍港。
4. 牆面隨河道變遷改變建材的有趣變化。

頭城車站以南

頭城職人故事展

N

5

9

吉祥路

9

⊙ 頭城火車站

頭城濱海路一段

2庚

5

6

5

2庚

4

⊙ 頂埔火車站

7

2

191甲

3

2

2

1

191甲

5

1. 《柔軟的內在》
2. 《風篤劇羽毛》
3. 《百魚圖 心中的顏色》
4. 《悲喜音，北管戲》
5. 《我們擁有的不僅黃昏》
6. 《忽然一夜清香發》
7. 《走遙遠的路》

車站以南

Toucheng Old Street

若是走北宜高下頭城交流道，往頭城而去，就是頭城車站以南的區域，省道兩旁有職人的工作室或店家，高速公路下就是 TBM park，是值得一遊的私房景點。

柔軟的內在
——芭樂甜心・林文亭

東北季風陣陣襲來，海風拂過蘭陽平原，水霧纏綿，氤氳濕氣在雪山山脈與中央山脈前停留腳步，籠罩沙質腹地。臺灣早期民眾多為務農，三十幾年前，頭城開始大量種植土芭樂，由於得天獨厚的地理位置，加上細心照料，芭樂擁有獨特的口感、香氣與味道，逐漸成為在地的特殊經濟作物。

身為返鄉青年，林文亭對於芭樂有一份深厚的情感。

大學就讀物流管理，畢業後至疊杯協會工作，再前往紐西蘭打工度假，從事農業相關工作。紐西蘭為農業大國，土地大，制度完善，組織管理有條不紊。這些經驗，在在影響林文亭對於家鄉果園的想法。返臺後先行進修，學習室內設計，特力屋工作三年後，決定返鄉務農，嘗試引進相關所學。農耕之餘，積極投入在地的社區策展與藝術創作，如壁畫、海廢藝術再生，以及參與馬祖藝術駐村。

「明明就是我原本的家，應該要更喜歡它。」返鄉主因，除了自然環境，更是為了

協助年長父母。頭城種植芭樂的農夫，大都七十歲以上，現存果農可能不到五十戶，栽種技術隨時可能產生巨大斷裂。

　　甜心芭樂，又稱鹽水月芭，屬於古老品種「中山月芭樂」。老一輩人常說「過鹽水」，指的是芭樂樹長期受到海風吹拂，果實自然而然吸收海霧的微

對於返鄉務農的林文亭而言，需要兼顧溝通與實踐。

量元素，因而孕育內在綿密、口感細緻的軟芭樂。外表翠綠，內裡則分為紅心芭樂和白心芭樂。早期頭城芭樂多為白心，現已有果農量產紅心。一年一收，集中夏季，前置作業得做管理照護；產期結束，工作量雖然大幅減少，亦得修剪枝葉刈除雜草。

> 由於得天獨厚的風土，頭城的芭樂，擁有獨特的口感、香氣與味道。

「我們最在乎的，就是吃得健康。」

承繼並沒有如此輕鬆。身為芭樂果農第三代，自我的想法時常跟長輩牴觸。林文亭表示，溝通非常重要，同時得準確實踐行動。代代之間其實相互依賴，老一輩需要新一代去拓展客源、導入宅配、賦予耕作全新釋義，新一代則需要老一輩的種植經驗。兩者互補，缺一不可。此外，對於耕作方式，亦有變動。早期蟲害嚴重，雜草叢生，需要不斷噴灑農藥；現代追求健康有機，採用新型耕作方式，引進最新科學技術，使用黑色抑制草蓆覆蓋果園便是其一。沙地悶熱，得注意保濕，覆蓋抑制草蓆除了可以節省人力，保持果園乾淨，更能讓雜草無法行光合作用，自然凋萎死亡，化為芭樂養分。同時，得細心照料果實，防止曬傷、椿象咬嚙、壓傷，以及各種蟲害等。

	2
1	---
	3

1 內在綿密、口感細緻的軟芭樂。（圖片提供：林文亭）

2 追求健康有機，使用黑色抑制草蓆覆蓋果園。

3 包裝禮盒也重新設計，提升芭樂的價值。

　　那幾乎是整體的審視、完整的介入，以及明確的行動。重新設計包裝禮盒，經營各種公開行銷管道，包含臉書、Line、經銷網頁等，甚至自行設計專屬的 Line 貼圖。積極聯繫客人，親踏果園，任一產銷環節，都見青年熱切投入散溢熱情的心力。

　　夏有雷雨，土地瀰漫濃濃芭樂果香，剖開來，細心呵護的一切，其實都有柔軟的內在。

■ ■ ■

Profile

頭城鎮農會輔導芭樂產銷班生產之甜心芭樂，產期在每年 7~9 月，栽培在沿海砂質礫土，果樹吸收太平洋鹽水霧氣中微量元素，果實風味獨特，果實成熟時呈金黃幸福顏色，果肉軟嫩，味道香甜。

用手機掃描QR code，深入認識頭城職日生

▲ 收聽訪談　　　　▲ 甜心芭樂

"This is my hometown, and I should love it more."

Lin Wen-ting is a young returnee to Toucheng, Yilan, who makes a living by growing guavas. She made the decision out of her love for guavas and nature, as well as her desire to look after her aging parents back home.

Lin Wen-ting:
Guava Farmer in Toucheng

Lin studied logistics management in college. After graduation, she went to New Zealand for a working holiday, doing agriculture-related work. New Zealand is an agricultural country with vast amounts of land and has a well-established management system. Lin gained extensive experience there, which later shaped her views on how to manage her family's orchard. After returning to Taiwan, she went on to study interior design and then worked for three years in TLW, one of Taiwan's leading home improvement retailers, before returning to Yilan to grow guavas and apply what she had learned over the years. In addition to being a guava farmer, Lin is an artist who actively engages in community curation and art activities. She enjoys painting murals and turning ocean trash into art pieces; she has also participated in the Matsu Artist Residency Program.

The guavas she grows are known as "sweet guavas," an ancient local variety in Toucheng, Yilan, characterized by their moon-like shape and tender meat. The unique texture of the guava is due to its constant exposure to the salt-laden sea breeze that blows through Toucheng. Sweet guavas are green on the outside and either white or red on the inside. In the early days, most farmers in Toucheng grew red guavas. Nowadays, both red and white guavas are grown. Sweet guavas are harvested once a year in summer. Before harvesting, proper care must be taken. After the harvest, though the workload is greatly reduced, pruning and mowing are still required.

So, come to Toucheng in summer and enjoy the sweet guava! When you cut it open, you see not only the soft flesh of the fruit but also the hard work of farmers who grow it despite the rain and thunderstorms.

風鳶刷羽毛

——四十甲溼地的守護者・蘭陽城鄉美學基金會

　　斯土斯民，在地再生，為了鄉土的長遠發展，我們究竟能夠展開怎樣的可能？不流於口號，不好高騖遠，捲起衣袖躬身參與。

　　蕭錫鑫，財團法人蘭陽城鄉美學基金會董事長，亦是頭城和風時尚 VILLA 會館董事長，來宜蘭生活、工作與打拚已 20 餘年，心懷願景，對於鄉鎮規劃有著長遠藍圖。表示自己身為社會一員，經營觀光企業有成，行有餘力理應反饋，成為一位慷慨的給予者。在此信念之下，大舉推動基金會，希望能**以企業之力，倡導環境教育、生態保育、城鄉美學等理念，促使地方成為一個更好的生活場域。**

　　基金會的主要活動，是以頭城四十甲溼地作為環境認養，此外，藉由各種系列活動，推廣生態保育，如植樹護樹、海洋淨灘、清除小花蔓澤蘭、自然生態志工研習、保育鳥類認識等。

　　蕭錫鑫表示，除了四十甲溼地，還在宜蘭各地進行沿線行道樹綠美化，以及環境維護相關管理，未來將持續拓展地域。目前的重點放在兩處：一，跑馬古道櫻花照護；二，針對礁溪一處 30 公頃苗圃進行生態復育。志工團隊中有多位教授，亦會結合課程，帶領青年學子施行在地養護，積極培育下一代。

經由數年努力，成果已然開枝散葉。行於溼地隧道，可見自在優游的黑面琵鷺、紫鷺、蒼鷺、夜鷺、白鷺等十餘種鳥類；其中，部分大型候鳥紫鷺，已從候鳥轉為留鳥，孵蛋繁衍，成為**全臺唯一可以欣賞紫鷺之美的地區。**

水域遼闊，不受汙染，豐富的自然生態，化身宜蘭環境保護、生態復育的示範基地。同時，因為民間力量的先行驅動，而使公部門關注此處區域，進而投注經費，加強硬體設施，美化公共空間。在此，公部門與私部門的彼此支援、相互協力，共同完成一種難能可貴的典範。

基金會中，有兩位長期付出的長青支柱，撐起

蕭錫鑫、蕭順德、高莉庭（由右到左）是基金會重要支柱。

志工服務的核心統籌。其一，蕭順德，現為蘭陽城鄉美學基金會頭城志工隊隊長，年近八十，身子仍顯精幹，精神矍鑠，步行極快，說起話來中氣十足。其二，則是人稱「麻吉姐」的高莉庭，退休之後，從臺北轉居頭城，現為志工隊總幹事，積極熱情，充滿活力，時刻面帶爽朗笑容，具有極強的號召力，一肩扛起活動的聯繫、通知與動員。

> 以基金會之力，倡導城鄉美學理念，促使地方成為一個更好的生活場域。

2018 年 5 月 3 日，基金會認養頭城四十甲地，正式揭牌，準備進行長期清潔。當初，排水溝布滿垃圾，由於周圍遍布魚塭，汙泥混雜大量魚骨、家庭垃圾，以及不知從何而來的事業廢棄物，志工團隊花費許多精力，才逐漸將地域修復成乾淨面貌。

如今，長期志工已有 80 餘位，每次參與清潔者大約有 40 到 50 位。晨早，天光初亮，一群安居頭城的長者，聚集頭城四十甲地租借而來的基地，分排貨櫃屋前領取器具。志工共分四組，三組兵分多路，持拿畚箕掃把負責掃除；第四組持拿長夾，撿拾全區垃圾；此外，視狀況增設機動組。每次打掃約 1 至 2 小時，由於效率佳，近年逐漸擴大清潔區域。

「你欲去抾（拾）糞埽（垃圾）無？」這是兩人問候親友的熱情方式。

1	2

1 值得守護的四十溋地。

2 志工們是四十甲溋地改頭換面的功臣。（圖片提供：蘭陽城鄉美學基金會）

因其長期付出，逐漸聚集一群志同道合、均已退休的長者，每個月兩次自發性清潔，無意間產生了多重意義，是行動守護，是節能減碳，亦是地方社群的噓寒問暖交際聯誼。為了生活所在，人文、環境與地域在此結合，匯成一股源源不絕的力量。

頭城下埔綠色隧道，現在已是一條名聞遐邇的自然步道。東側是寬敞魚塭，迎接太平洋陣陣海風，西側是平原腹地，遠眺雪山遠近山脊，這裡曾被社會棄置，被認為是瀰漫惡臭骯髒汙穢之地，如今綠蔭夾道，行人帶著孩子三三兩兩悠閒散步，將一條路走過一次又一次。

風鳶刷羽毛，鳥喙啄翠綠，正是因為這一群風雨無阻的長者，挽起衣袖，揮汗撿拾，做一位真正的行動者，而使整個地方產生巨大改變，這一切都不嫌晚——願我們都能如此，踏出腳步，彎腰低頭，再次學習生命的謙卑。

...

Profile

財團法人蘭陽城鄉美學基金會成立於 2018 年 4 月 16 日，至今，每個月仍然固定舉辦志工清潔，單月雙次，從不停歇，持續自發維護自然環境，成為積極行動的楷模。

用手機掃描QR code，
深入認識頭城職日生

▲臉書粉專

Xiao Xi-xin is the CEO of Lan-Yang Urban-Rural Aesthetics Foundation and He-fong Villa. As a member and a successful businessman in the tourism industry, he believes he should give back to society and

Protectors of
the Wetland Area in Xiapu, Toucheng

sees it as his responsibility to do so. Years ago, he set up long-term plans to support local development in Yilan and founded the Lan-Yang Urban-Rural Aesthetics Foundation, a social enterprise, to promote environmental education, ecological conservation, and urban-rural aesthetics, with hopes of making Yilan a better place to live in.

One of the foundation's main missions is to maintain the cleanliness of the wetland area in Xiapu, Toucheng, or the 40-jia Wetland area, on a long-term basis. The foundation pledged to protect it through regular cleaning activities on May 3, 2018, and the cleaning project is now led by two important figures of the foundation—Xiao Shun-de, leader of the volunteer team, and Gao Li-ting, the executive secretary.

Today, there are more than 80 long-term volunteers engaging in this cleaning project, many of whom are gray-haired local residents. They voluntarily join the cleaning activities that take place about twice a month—around 40-50 people participating each time. Early in the morning, or more specifically 6:00 in summer or 6:30 in winter, they gather at a rented site in the wetland area and go in groups to collect cleaning tools at a container shed. By participating in cleaning activities, they not only make practical contributions to local environmental protection but also continue to deepen their friendship with each other, forming a cohesive force that can bring a positive impact to the local community.

Thanks to the elderly volunteers who roll up their sleeves to clean up the environment rain or shine, the once dirty and smelly wetland area is now clean and beautiful, boasting a well-known picturesque tree-lined trail, where birds sing and leaves rustle in the breeze. It's never too late to join the ranks of environmental protection and make contributions to society—let's all take this step forward and make it our mission to work towards a better community, with a respectful attitude towards nature and life.

《百魚圖》：心中的顏色

——船老大的畫筆下有百魚船・陳正勝

「咱的祖先以前就共咱警告矣，咱以後就是：有海討甲（到）無海，有魚掠（抓）甲無魚。其實猶（還）會赴（來得及）啦，你對這馬（現在）開始，你共保護啊。」

如果攝影是面向世界，進行寫實拓印的復刻，那麼船老大陳正勝的百魚繪畫，則以形象描摹作為基礎，肆意揮灑，野放色彩，完成內心流動的精神光影。一幅一幅畫作，魚群湧生，波浪層疊，展現大海的寬廣容納；同時，彰顯人與魚獨特的雙向浸潤。人的細髮幻化魚的肉身，魚的眼睛映照人的神情，那是輪廓、色澤與浮想聯翩的夢幻世界，仰賴通感，再生心之所向的海洋。

船老大陳正勝，1956 年生，長於漁村，以海為伍，熱愛魚類，從小堅定志向，**希望未來的工作、生活與志業，永不背離海洋**。就讀基隆海事，考取航海證照，跑了數年遠洋，直到 26 歲時兒子出生，才決定從海上歸返。1985 年開設正勝釣具，經營海釣船。1988 年至 1995 年，成為臺灣釣魚雜誌的特派記者，撰寫魚類相關專欄。愛魚的船老大，時常將櫃子、牆壁、抽屜、冰箱、釣具箱等作為畫布，畫下各種熟識如親密友朋的魚群。2011 年，由於察覺海洋資源日漸凋零，決定收起釣具店和海釣船。

船老大筆下所繪是對魚隻的熟稔、鍾愛與記憶，下圖為工作室一隅。

首張魚圖，是《紅目魚鰱》。

2013 年，正式用廣告漆畫魚，在 FB 成立「船老大的魚世界」，分享畫作，製作短片，介紹近乎失傳的魚類相關俗諺，解釋各種魚類的真實習性、典故及傳說。近期最為重要的作品，當屬 2017 年至 2020 年完成的《百魚圖》全系列，由 69 幅畫作組成，長 69 尺，高 85 公分，意欲藉此藝術創作，喚醒社會大眾對於海洋的

> 素人畫家繪百魚，描摹形象後，肆意揮灑色彩，完成內心流動的精神光影。

生態關懷。此外，作品還有《討海人的最佳海味》、《最毒的魚類》、《最好吃的魚類》、《海底十二生肖》、《人、魚、野獸》等系列作品。或可指稱，這些畫風大膽不拘色彩的畫作，除了展現令人驚異的天賦，更存有一份深切關注，諭示未來竭澤而漁的匱乏。

「我會一直畫，畫到海底沒有魚。」

作為一位素人畫家，船老大或許不曾揣摩藝術作品的學派畫風，筆下所繪，除了是對魚隻的熟稔、鍾愛與記憶，更是精神的自在空間，是自我對大海的眷戀，是《老人與海》的相互關係。顏色不拘，人魚易位，每一滴水滴彷彿都具有靈性。「眾多魚中，最喜歡曼波魚，因為自由自在不拘小節，像是自己在畫圖時隨心所欲將內心的顏色表現出來。」

1

1 陳正勝筆下的魚世界，熱情且自由。（圖片提供：陳正勝）

　　畢卡索的話語：「我花了四年時間，畫得像拉斐爾一樣，但用了一輩子的時間，才能像孩子一樣畫畫。」船老大陳正勝的畫作中，藏隱童真，洋溢熱情，是不受限制的真正自由，有著野獸派用色的大膽鮮豔，有著超現實主義的夢幻奇想，以及原始藝術的不假修飾內心直觀。

　　我們在其作品，與其說是看見一位素人畫家歷經沉潛，最終爆發繪畫才能，不如說是看見一位秉持初心，持續面向已然僵化的世界，細筆描摹毫無遮蔽的自然，自然而然給予顏色、線條與迷人輪廓。那所蘊含，不僅是藝術，更是一位藉由畫作，闡述環境倫理與生命教育的倡議者。

■ ■ ■

Profile

素人藝術家陳正勝先生，人稱「船老大」，2017 年開始繪畫《百魚圖》。以各種魚的圖案，意圖連結海洋、人和魚之間的關係，這是藝術的表達，亦是對於大海與生命的尊重。

用手機掃描QR code，深入認識頭城職日生

▲ 收聽訪談　　　▲ 臉書粉專

"I will keep painting until there are no fish in the sea."

Chen Zheng-sheng:
Sea Captain with a Passion for **Painting**

Growing up in a fishing village, Captain Chen Zheng-sheng has long developed a deep love for fish and a strong connection with the ocean. He knew from a very young age that the sea would be an integral part of his life, and this has become the driving force behind his career and life choices. He attended the Affiliated Keelung Maritime Senior High School of National Taiwan Ocean University, obtained his navigating license, and spent years sailing on the open ocean until his son was born when he was 26, prompting him to return to land. In 1985, he opened a fishing tackle shop and started to take customers out for sea fishing. From 1988 to 1995, he worked as a special correspondent for Taiwan Fishing Magazine, covering fish-related topics.

Chen sees fish as his good friends, and he likes to paint them on all kinds of surfaces, such as drawers, walls, fridges, fishing tackle PEOPLEes, and more. In 2013, he started to use advertisement paint for painting, and in the same year, he created a Facebook fan page called "Old Captain's Fish World," where he often shares his paintings and uploads short clips introducing the habits of different fishes, some nearly lost fish-related idioms, anecdotes, legends, etc.

His most prominent recent painting work is the "Hundreds of Fishes" series, consisting of 69 paintings together measuring 69 meters in length and 85 centimeters in height. The series was created from 2017 to 2020 with the aim of raising marine environmental awareness among the public. His other painting works include "Best Seafood for Fishermen," "Most Poisonous Fish," "Most Delicious Fish," "Twelve Marine Creatures: Contrasting with the Twelve Chinese Zodiac Animals," "Human, Fish, and Beast," and more. Characterized by the bold and unconventional use of color, his works showcase his amazing talent and his deep concern for the overconsumption of ocean resources.

From his works, one can tell that he is more than a gifted painter gradually refining his skills over time, but an artist who, in a world where nature is increasingly being neglected and undervalued, insists on depicting the most authentic and captivating beauty of the sea and its living inhabitants. With vibrant colors, various lines, and captivating contours, his paintings are not only a feast for the eyes but also a call to action for environmental education, sustainability, and responsibility.

悲喜音，北管戲

在地產業

——讓北管風采在頭城昂揚・陳玉環

廟埕的戲棚，酬神的舞臺，燦爛燈光八方閃爍，藝師伴著北管樂器兩側待命，伶人穿著氣派華服正準備粉墨登場。

曾有論言，宜蘭文化三寶為傀儡戲、歌仔戲和北管戲，漢陽北管劇團即佔兩項。頭城與羅東曾是北管重鎮，鼎盛時期，鄰里村落擁有各自的北管陣頭。北管陣頭與北管戲不同，北管陣頭專指婚喪喜慶、神明祭典的伴奏樂團；北管戲則由北管搭配戲曲，籠統包含子弟戲和亂彈戲，前者由業餘的軒社登臺，後者由專業的戲班演出。

1988 年，臺灣戲曲樂師莊進才在羅東成立漢陽歌劇團。2002 年，易名「漢陽北管劇團」。2000 年起，多次榮獲宜蘭縣傑出演藝團隊。2008 年，行政院文建會指定為重要傳統藝術北管戲曲類保存團體。2009 年，獲宜蘭縣登錄無形文化資產。2016 年，由莊進才學生陳玉環接任團長。現為全國唯一職業北管劇團，主要的展演形式，為「日演北管、夜演歌仔 / 北管」。

悲喜之音，北管日夜演奏；忠孝之戲，北管戲細膩演繹。

「這是來自故鄉的深沉聲音。」陳玉環老家位於
二城國小正門口，比鄰省道青雲路二段。北管陣頭
曾經日復穿行，那是出殯的傷逝之路，是嫁娶的喜
慶之路，更是神明出巡佳節慶典的必經之路。對於
陳玉環而言，北管的昂揚激越，音質的高亢喧闐，
以及流露其中的滄桑抑鬱，是一整個時代的精神記
憶。陳玉環特別指出，如同法國的「世界偶戲節」
揚名國際，宜蘭在地的北管與北管戲，具有無可取
代的文化藝術價值。

　　整體而言，北管與北管戲式微得相當嚴重，自
陳入門有其難度，表面不甚討喜、難以親近，然而
理解之後，便能發現蘊藏其中的美學。身為劇團團

陳玉環期待頭城能夠再次
展現北管風采。

115

長，作為主要推廣者，對於傳承責無旁貸，初始略顯保守，不善與人盤摑；經由不斷調整，開始懂得主動出擊，果敢表達想法大聲呼籲。陳玉環由衷坦言，訴求未被重視，劇團更不曾在頭城的搶孤、音浪與千龜來朝等大型活動，擁有表演機會；沮喪之餘，並不氣餒，因為陳玉環知道恆常的努力，不僅是為了劇團的留存、名聲的遠揚，更是為了蘭陽傳統文化的傳承、發展與續命。

> 宜蘭在地的北管與北管戲，具有無可取代的文化藝術價值，傳承是當務之急。

任何藝術，無不期待長年積累的遺產，能夠有所傳承。對其內部，漢陽北管劇團積極培育下一代，在文化資產局傳習計畫的輔助下，聘請資深團員作為授課藝師，一步一腳印，引領新進藝生中青團員。無論前場扮戲，或是後場伴奏，藝生除了定期排練之外，亦會逐漸參與民戲、傳藝與校園戲曲推廣等公開表演，期許在這過程之中，逐漸積攢經驗，終而獨當一面予以承繼。

1	2

1 每一場演出與其過程，都將是珍貴的歷史遺產。

2 演出的前期準備、排練現場，是重要的傳承所在。

　　對於未來，陳玉環期待頭城能夠再次展現北管風采，同時希望公部門能夠主動舉辦北管比賽，設立獎勵，無論給予獎金，或者承諾表演機會；漢陽北管劇團可以作為展演示範，化身國樂與傳統戲曲的前導掌舵。藉由活動，讓民眾有更多機會接觸北管與北管戲，大幅拉近距離。重要的是，這些難能可貴的演出機會，俾使團員能有相對穩定的生活；此外，演出的前期準備、當下演出與後期檢討，更是重要的傳承現場，對於觀賞者和劇團成員而言，都將產生彌足珍貴的經驗。

　　戲臺上下，北管左右，拉開序幕的不僅是一齣戲，更是示現每一自我，對於故鄉傳統文化的認識、涵養與認同。此外，關於真實的人生，我們看見陳玉環堅守北管／北管戲，竭力奮戰，而那無疑是另一齣更為隆重的華麗大戲。

＿＿＿＿

Profile

漢陽北管劇團是宜蘭最具代表性的民間傳統劇團，也是國內唯一專業職業北管劇團。1988 年成立於羅東，為發揚及保存宜蘭特有之北管戲曲，秉持「日演北管、夜演歌仔」，讓北管戲曲於民間持續發聲。

用手機掃描QR code，深入認識頭城職日生

▲收聽訪談　　▲臉書粉專

Hanyang Beiguan Troupe (formerly known as Hanyang Opera Troupe before 2002) was founded by Zhuang Jin-cai, a renowned Taiwanese traditional opera musician, in Lu-odong, Yilan, in 1988. Since 2000, the troupe

Chen Yu-huan:
Head of Hanyang Beiguan Troupe

has been awarded Outstanding Performing Arts Group in Yilan multiple times. In 2008, the troupe was designated as a preserver of important traditional arts under the category of Beiguan Music by the Council for Cultural Affairs (now known as the Ministry of Culture), Executive Yuan, and in 2009, it was regis-tered as an "Intangible Cultural Heritage" by the Yilan County. As the only professional Beiguan troupe in Taiwan, Hanyang Beiguan Troup is currently led by Zhuang Jin-cai's stu-dent, Chen Yu-huan, who took over as the head in 2016. Typically, the troupe performs Beiguan music and opera during the day and Taiwanese Opera at night.

"Beiguan music is the sound of my hometown." Chen, a native of Toucheng, used to live right across from the entrance of the Ercheng Elementary School, adjacent to Section 2 of Qingyun Road—a frequent route for funeral and wedding processions, as well as religious parades. As Chen recalled, the sound of Beiguan music and chen-t'ou was often heard as they passed by. For Chen, Beiguan music is lively, energetic, and boisterous, but at the same time nostalgic and wistful; it carries the memories of a bygone era in Taiwan. She noted that Beiguan music and Beiguan opera in Yilan have irreplaceable cultural and artistic value, like the art of puppetry in France, which gained international recognition through the World Festival of Puppet Theatres.

Expecting and hoping that Beiguan music and Beiguan opera can regain their former glory in Toucheng and that more people can become familiar with them through event participation, Chen called on the government to proactively organize competitions and grant awards—whether it be prize money or performance opportunities. She also expressed Hanyang Beiguan Troupe's willingness to do demonstration performances, taking the lead in reviving the traditional art form of Beiguan.

Chen has been fighting hard to revive Beiguan music and Beiguan opera throughout her life. Her story is just as compelling as any spectacular stage play—but holds even greater significance.

文化教育

我們擁有的不僅黃昏
——少年的廟宇文化王・梁鈜傑

　　青年的昂然，倨傲的神色，心中卻彷彿住著歷經世事的老靈魂。一言一行，無比篤定，展現常人難以具備的行動力——這是由鄉土餵哺長大的孩子，吹奏北管，自學民俗刺繡，往返陣頭之中，乃至將其所學於焉反饋。

　　梁鈜傑，2000 年出生，從宜蘭高商多媒體設計科畢業，現就讀佛光大學文化資產與創意學系四年級。就學期間，因其對地方文化的熟稔，而被老師稱為「文化王」。

　　從小，阿公帶著梁鈜傑接觸頭城民俗活動，包含搶孤、放水燈、神明生日慶典等，不知不覺受到宗教文化的潤澤。早期，宜蘭有上百個北管樂團，現在大約只剩三、四十團，每團不逾十人，老化凋零，出團還得相互支援。頂埔有兩團北管子弟，人數極少。2016 年暑假，梁鈜傑自尋耆老支持，懇請劉建旺老師傅開班授課，**傳承北管技藝，意圖重振「頂埔集蘭社」**。

　　現代社會的生活型態劇烈改變，早期以廟宇作為活動中心，民眾無不熱切參與，增添熱鬧；如今重心轉移，北管遂從群聚分享，演變成為鄉里間的高分貝噪音。頂埔集蘭社北管的練習地點，一路從頂埔活動中心轉移至噶瑪蘭

梁鈜傑期許自己傳承
北管技藝，重振「頂埔
集蘭社」。

救難協會竹安據點，再轉移至竹安河口，現在落腳
頭城青雲路一段三圍橋底下。輪胎駛過橋墩，猴洞
坑溪從旁汩汩流過，嗩吶聲響的張揚，兀自洋溢一
種蒼老哀傷的氣質。團練少了，課程斷了，然而熱
愛北管之心未曾中止，還在不斷尋找合適的練習地
點。

　　梁鈜傑不曾停留於口號。長期參與陣頭，對於
使用的旗幟、壓帆樣式不甚滿意，有了學習宗教刺
繡的念頭；2021 年初，新冠肺炎疫情爆發，學校改
為遠距上課，多了大量時間，梁鈜傑開始**自主學習
宗教刺繡**。走訪民間繡莊，實地觀看老師傅技藝，
點滴學習，然而由於缺乏系統教育，須從謬誤中不

停揣摩，從錯誤中不斷修正。訂製「繡規」（立形繡架），購買刺繡原料「蔥布」，一切從頭開始。初始，一天刺繡五小時，後來時常從中午十二點工作至半夜十二點。第一件作品是「彰化太子堂頭旗」，緩慢摸索，花了半年才得以完成。第二件作品是「臺東大慶玉石頭旗」，時間已縮短至兩個月。現今，刺繡技藝日臻熟練，逐漸發展自我風格。

> 他吹奏北管，自學民俗刺繡，
> 往返陣頭之中，撐起子弟團，
> 承襲宮廟民俗技藝。

「配色」與「圖稿」，是梁鈜傑對於刺繡成品最為得意之處。每件作品，無不廣泛參考前人樣式，吸收各地特色圖騰，添加自身想法，考量成品的角度、顏色、前後起伏感等，具體彰顯孕育於在地生活的美感。色彩鮮活，不顯雜亂，呈現自主核心。

「將作品展示出來，心中有股驕傲的感覺，自己死後，作品還能不斷流傳下去。」2022 年頂埔順天府四年一次繞境，恰逢集蘭社 90 週年紀念，是以盛大參與，總共號召三百人加入，出動大鼓亭、金龍團、北管、大仙尪仔，另有頭旗、彩牌、自製的六面牛舌旗和一面壓帆共同

1 帶領更多年輕人熱情投入與行動，找回屬於子弟團的驕傲。

2 短短時日，梁鈜傑刺繡技藝日臻熟練，並發展自我風格。

3 宮廟與陣頭文化永遠能振奮人心。

慶賀。梁鈜傑表示，那是生命中無比激動的時刻，即使地方宮廟民俗技藝日漸萎縮，陣頭文化走向凋零，他還是以自己的熱情、投入與行動，向我們展示**民間宗教所能給予的，絕非昏瞶的文化黃昏。**

　　那一張倨傲、頑強且露出微笑的臉，原來正是因為，堅決承襲文化，勇敢挺立土地的姿態。

Profile

頂埔集蘭社為宜蘭頭城頂埔庄子弟團，成立約於昭和7年，因社員逐漸老化凋零，2016 年由在地青年重振，並以新時代的方式傳承下去。

用手機掃描QR code，深入認識頭城職日生

▲收聽訪談　　▲臉書粉專

Liang is currently a senior in the Department of Cultural Assets and Reinvention at Fo Guang University, Yilan. He started to participate in various folk events in Toucheng with his grandfather at a very young age, such as the Qianggu Festival, the Water Lantern Festival, and birthday celebrations of the gods. Without realizing it, he slowly developed a strong interest in religious culture.

Liang Hong-jie:
Inheritor & **Promoter** of
Temple Culture (Beiguan & Religious Embroidery)

According to Liang, there used to be over a hundred Beiguan (a type of traditional Chinese music often played at weddings, funerals, and religious processions) troupes in Yilan, but now there are only 30 to 40 left, each with less than ten members and all facing a serious aging problem. As a result, to put on a performance, they often need to "borrow" performers from other troupes. Determined to preserve Beiguan culture and revive the long-established Beiguan troupe, "Ding-Pu Ji-Lan Club," Liang took the initiative in the summer of 2016 to visit the elderly and earnestly requested Liu

Jian-wang to hold classes and teach Beiguan skills.

In addition to Beiguan, Liang has a strong interest in religious embroidery. This interest was planted in his mind long ago after participating in chen-t'ou (a parade tradition in Taiwan) for years and seeing that some embroidered flag designs could be further improved upon. As a man of action, Liang followed through with his intent in the beginning of 2021 when schools switched to remote learning due to COVID-19, giving him a lot more extra time. He started to learn religious embroidery on his own bit by bit, as well as visiting local embroidery shops to observe the skills of the masters in person and constantly correcting and learning from his mistakes.

He bought a standing embroidery frame and embroidery fabric so that he could practice embroidery—initially five hours a day and later often from noon to midnight. He spent a lot of time exploring while doing his first embroidery work, the head flag for Changhua Tai Zih Temple, which eventually took him six months to complete. For his second work, the head flag for Taitung Daqing Jade Development Co., Ltd., he significantly reduced the time spent to two months. Today, his embroidery skills have become even more proficient and he has gradually developed his own style.

From Liang, we see the vitality and confidence of a young man whose words and actions reveal determination and extraordinary proactivity. As he tirelessly dedicates himself to Beiguan and religious embroidery, actively engages in traditional parades of chen-t'ou, and constantly makes his best effort to contribute to his hometown, he seems to possess the mindset of an experienced old soul. A young native of Toucheng, he is definitely an inheritor and promoter of temple culture in Taiwan.

忽然一夜清香發

在地產業

— 延續手工製香技藝與記憶・林建宏

　　早年，頭城的金盈、金面和頂埔里，是「剖香腳（製作香心）」的重鎮，地方子弟時常學習相關技藝，是重要的在地產業。己文堂最初的工廠亦在頂埔里，位於頭城頂埔王爺廟旁，茲因腹地不大，空間受限，決定另覓他處。林建宏的父親小學畢業後，開始當學徒，學做香，後來工廠出現狀況尋求頂讓，父親請叔叔回來一起創業。「己文堂」之名，分別取自林建宏的父親與叔叔名字各一字，合為品牌名稱，代表兄弟齊心打拚。

　　臺灣的手工製香業，原是自立工廠，後來為了賺取高額利潤，尋求低廉薪資而陸續外移。1980年代，工廠開始大量移至中國大陸，再遷至越南，最後落腳泰國和柬埔寨。如今，在地的手工製香產業，近乎絕跡。己文堂製香，遵循古法，要求整支立香純屬天然，不願沾染其他雜粉，不願羼雜其他香精化工原料，有其不可更易的堅持。無可諱言，手工製香的成本高昂，初階評估似乎不存在競爭力，然而好香的價值，正逐漸被市場肯定。

　　林建宏，己文堂製香廠第二代傳人。原先學習武術，就讀文化大學體育系，畢業後成為武術教練。父親並無要求繼承，然而，卻能感受阿爸心中的深深期望，返回家鄉，嘗試接管家業。從最底層的員

林建宏除了傳承香的製作，更希望能建立系統性的香學教育。

工做起，認真研習每一項製香技術，親自跑業務，取得原料——那絕非一件容易之事。

　　白日勤跑業務，學習待人接物；夜晚沉潛專業知識，包含調香的步驟，認識樹種特性等。原先不辨香味差異，經過數年積累，才習得調香與製香能力。當時雪隧未通，宜蘭臺北來往都得經由北宜九彎十八拐，跑完業務已是深夜，疲倦不堪，時常停在石碇休息幾個小時，再回頭城。正式管理家業前，心中亦存雜音，不知自己是否適合，然而在緩慢的摸索學習之中，開始逐漸確立核心價值。

　　「處事和產品要做好，必須言行合一，要先有精神價值，才能延續與傳承。」父親的叮嚀，始終言猶在耳。

早期原料，大多來自原料供應商，購買現成木粉，只是品質不均，容易摻混其他雜粉。即使親臨產地，廠商的運作模式都是先購買後送貨。訂購後送至頭城，已是四、五個月之後，木頭品質可能產生變化。木頭若是不佳，直接影響香的品質，必然無法使用，進而造成資金無謂損失。再者，購買木頭至研磨廠加工，亦有可能摻雜其他木粉，質地仍然不穩。

> **產品遵循古法，要求整支立香純屬天然；處事要先有精神價值，才能延續與傳承。**

如今，增加新設備，請廠商直送原料至工廠，再依照木頭品質與販售價格進行評估，購買樣品一、兩百公斤，先行試用，符合預期再進貨櫃。自行購入原木，機器壓碎，使木材成為小碎片與小顆粒狀，放入研磨機，再將細粉置入攪拌機，過篩的木粉原料才會一致，香氣才能均衡。

一支好香，除了依靠香木、植物花果所製的香粉提升價值，更須憑藉線香十二道製程，以及無數次的挑選與試驗才能完成。工法繁複，分別由三輪的沾、附、展和掄等技巧組成，得恃多年經驗才能養成上手。林建宏笑著說：「如果認真做這十二道工法的話，可能一個小時手就會開始發抖了。」

「香藥同源」，每一種味道都有各自的獨特性，對於

身心靈都有不同影響，有些能夠幫助轉換情緒，有些能使身體鎮靜舒緩，有些則能增加活力，產地不同，氣味也就不同。林建宏除了承繼古法，製作單方香（純檀香和純沉香）和複方香（加入中藥），更學習西方精油等相關知識，以前主要是以草根類或木質類作為香氣主軸，現在嘗試添加花香，例如玫瑰、薰衣草和迷迭香等。**香不再只是信仰用香，不再單純局限宗教場合，更能滲入日常生活。**

己文堂近年推廣生活用香概念。生活用香，亦有多種產品形式，例如常見的立香，乃至臥香、環香、元寶香、香塔等，香所闡釋的氣味、氛圍以及日常的儀式感，經由嗅覺導引，漸次放鬆身體，賦予一種靜默似的療癒。此外，同知名陶瓷家兆博合作，聯名開發能夠放置香的陶瓷碟。

為了推廣香文化，己文堂提供工廠見習，民眾可以透過預約，由專人導覽，體驗製香流程。對於未來，林建宏想要建立系統性的香學教育，介紹香、香史和薰香應用，有意成立香史文學館。從林建宏身上，我們可以看到製香產業的傳承、轉型與創新，同時，更能看見一位香之子民的多年堅持。

忽然一夜清香發，原來我們，都必須從熟悉的故土出發。

▪▪▪

Profile

己文堂，全臺最大的手工製香廠，創始人林己能以推廣香的價值做為使命，目前傳承至第二代，依然堅持純正手工製香技術。曾被頭城頂埔順天府選中，製作重達 3000 公斤的天香，2009 年榮獲「國家優良品質獎」。

用手機掃描QR code，深入認識頭城瞱日生

▲收聽訪談　　▲臉書粉專

In the early days, Toucheng was a hub of incense production in Taiwan, boasting numerous factories, particularly in the villages of Jinying, Jinmian, and Dingpu. Lin Ji-neng,

Lin Jian-hong:
Present-Day Owner of the Incense-Making Store Ji Wen Tang

a Toucheng native, took on an apprenticeship in the incense-making trade upon completing his elementary school education. When the incense factory he worked in closed down, he approached his brother, Lin Wen-qin, with the idea of starting their own incense business. Together, they founded "Ji Wen Tang"—the "Ji" and "Wen" in the name of the store are a Chinese character taken from each of their names, symbolizing the idea that the brothers are working together as one.

Lin Ji-neng's son, Lin Jian-hong, is the second-generation inheritor of "Ji Wen Tang." At first, he planned to pursue a career in martial arts and knew almost nothing about incense making, first working as a martial arts instructor after graduating from the Department of Physical Education at Chinese Culture University. However, upon realizing his father's ardent desire for him to take over the family business, he voluntarily returned home to learn the family trade. Starting from the bottom, he devoted himself to learning every aspect of making incense, from raw material acquisition to manufacturing. During the day, he made a dedicated effort in sales, honing his abilities in dealing with customers. At night, he immersed himself in acquiring incense-making expertise, such as fragrance-blending techniques, and learning about the properties of different tree species. After several years of honing the necessary skills, he developed the mastery of fragrance blending and incense making, despite initially struggling to distinguish between different scents.

Incense holds significance not only in spiritual beliefs but also in people's daily lives. In Chinese medicine, incense is regarded as a form of "medicine." Each incense has its own scent and can have different effects on a person's mind, body, and spirit. Some can help shift emotions, some can help calm and soothe the body, and some can help increase vitality.

Incenses from different regions have different scents. What does the incense from your hometown smell like?

文化教育

走遙遠的路——馬偕行腳說頭城・陳順福

「你出去那麼久怎麼都沒跟我說？門前的盆栽都沒人澆水，我幫你澆了。」

日頭斜照，薄薄水霧波光瀲灩，一陣山風，一陣海浪，一條一條明顯隱匿的路，行至彼方，其實早已跨越盡頭。依循前人腳步，踏出確立的方向，風聲颯颯，福哥帶領我們面向海岸，述說百年前的馬偕故事，述說頭城早已消隱的噶瑪蘭部落故事，述說河道更易的歷史故事。聲線沉穩，個性內斂，踏出的每一個腳步，彷彿都在演繹行者的奧義。

陳順福不知命運會帶他來到這裡。

36 歲，當時已在臺北經營室內設計事務所數年，娶妻生子，購車買房，事業一帆風順，絕對是社會普遍意義上的成功人士。然而，日夜加班應酬，陪廠商吃飯喝酒，生活著實消磨，久而久之，健康出現警訊。

一次應酬隔日，妻子說，昨晚回家不僅嘔出食物，還大量吐血。這次經驗，讓陳順福真正開始重新審視自我，思考是否存有另一種生活可能。準備了將近一年，決定收掉公司，正式遷居宜蘭。離開臺北，先至礁溪，再至壯圍長居十年，最後輾轉落居頭城。

　　頭城的生活，讓陳順福再次感受人與人之間的
連結，那是日常的舉動，包含鄰人熱心替盆栽澆水，
或在門口置放一把新鮮青蔥等。

　　陳順福在頭城和平街南端買下屋宅，進行翻

陳順福得知馬偕事蹟後，
便開始整理移動路線，自
主進行實地踏查。

修，創立「小鎮生活」，那是一個親切的公共空間，向遊客、社區與民眾開放。簡單的桌椅，一面書櫃，牆壁懸掛馬偕入蘭行醫的文字介紹與相關照片，亦在此處舉辦演講與藝文展覽等。此外，擺設惜福冰箱，藉由食物共享，加強人與社區的連結。2022年，為了支持在地產業，原址現已由他人承租，轉型為「蘭城雨啡」特色咖啡店，容納紙塑藝術，並且作為文藝展演空間。

> 面向海岸，述說百年前的馬偕故事，走讀之間，以自我的行腳向前人致敬。

「現在的人，活得沒有比過去的人快樂。」

人們生活在資本主義之中，精神狀態卻日漸貧瘠，如此省察，應是近年自主推動「馬偕行腳——走路説故事」的主要原因。陳順福的遷居，巧妙呼應馬偕自1873年起，前往宜蘭行醫傳教的移動路線。對於陳順福而言，**遷居宜蘭，提供了前所未有的時間空間，得以放慢速度，專注生活，自在步入在地。**當他得知馬偕事蹟，便開

1　2

1 走在山間海岸，才懂篳路藍縷。（圖片提供：陳順福）

2 藉由走讀，讓多人認識人與土地的故事。（圖片提供：陳順福）

始閱覽相關書籍，整理百年前的移動路線，自主進行實地踏查。

遙遠的呼召，其實是迎面而來的精神領受。

緩調行踏，內向探索，自然再次回到生活之中。山風海浪，大地陪伴，療癒有傷的過往，重新面對純粹的自我，生命因而有了深沉轉變——這是馬偕的故事，是福哥的故事，是人與土地的故事，更是每一位躬身行者的故事。英國作家吉卜林所言：「他會在暮色時分回頭望著那些雄偉的山脈，以及沿途走來逐漸變得模糊細長的道路；他懷著山民慷慨開闊的眼界擬定隔日的全新旅程。」

依循前人路線，以自我的行腳致敬，彷彿如此，才能走出自己真正的路。

...

__Profile__

「馬偕行腳——走路說故事」是希望跟隨馬偕行腳的足跡，走讀一段頭城的小旅行，感受馬偕當初的心情；藉由途中觀察與思考，認識鄉土，觀照自己，讓馬偕精神繼續在地蔓延。

用手機掃描QR code，深入認識頭城職日生

▲收聽訪談　　▲臉書粉專

Chen Shun-fu is a tour guide in Yilan known for planning the "MacKay Travel" itinerary. By guiding tourists along the coastline and route taken by Dr. MacKay a hundred

Chen Shun-fu:
Tour Guide Who Planned the
MacKay Travel Itinerary

years ago and sharing stories about the doctor, the Kavalan Tribe that once resided in Toucheng, and how river courses have changed over time, he helps everyone to truly appreciate the natural and cultural beauty of Yilan.

For Chen, becoming a tour guide in Yilan was the result of an unexpected turn in his life. He started his career as an interior designer, and by age 36, he had his own interior design firm. However, he was not content with his life despite the business success he'd achieved. In addition, overworking and heavy social drinking had caused him to experience serious health problems, prompting him to rethink what kind of life he wanted to live. Later, he decided to close down his company and move to Yilan. After nearly a year of planning and preparation, he made it happen.

After moving to Yilan, Chen found himself with a lot more free time on his hands, allowing him to slow down the pace of daily life, explore local sights, and enjoy life. When he learned that Dr. MacKay had visited Yilan many times, he began searching through books and gathering information about the places he had been to. After checking them out in person, he planned out the "MacKay Travel" itinerary.

Just as Dr. MacKay took the route a hundred years ago, now with Chen's guidance, tourists can walk along the same route—into the mountains and along the coastline. With the wind and waves as company along the way, visitors can pay homage to Dr. MacKay as they immerse themselves in nature and embark on a journey of self-discovery, seek inner peace to heal the wounds of the past, and reflect on the path they truly want to take in the future.

沉睡於雪山隧道下的功臣

帶路人
講故事

陳碧琳

中原大學設計學
博士，現任宜蘭
縣立蘭陽博物館
館長。

TBM Park 位於雪隧南口附近，國道五號頭城段高架橋下，一架長達百餘公尺的大型機械靜靜地坐落，擁有歷盡風霜而鏽蝕的表面，它是建造雪隧的功臣之一——雪隧導坑 TBM「北宜一號」。

雪山隧道於 2006 年順利通車，是國道 5 號高速公路建設中最艱難的工程，除了工程的技術難題，更是以集體意志力對抗大自然反撲的艱苦歷程，足以躋身全球「最艱鉅建築工程」之列，大英百科全書也收錄了雪山隧道工程。

雪隧開挖時引進了挖掘英法海峽的 TBM（全斷面隧道鑽掘機）工法，運用有削岩鑽頭的機具 TBM 挖掘，從鑽頭、機身、輸送碴料的設施等，其總長度達 170 公尺，雪隧通車後，TBM 功成身退並拆解出坑，本要報廢，零件被堆置在國五頭城高架橋下，宜蘭縣政府爭取留存，為「臺灣最大的工程文物」。「北宜一號」不只是功成

身退的冰冷鋼材機件，而是具有人性溫度的紀念碑。

　　TBM 公園附近還有雪隧文物館、猴洞坑瀑布、己文堂、親子公園、林朝宗古厝、四十甲溼地，這些人文自然景點很少於網路上出現，可以說是頭城私房景點。（口述／陳碧琳，文字／簡云閒）

1. 陳碧琳推薦大家來參觀「臺灣最大的工程文物」。**2.** TBM 公園將報廢機械轉變成公共藝術。**3.** TBM 公園使國道五號高架橋下成為城市文物館的一部分。**4.** 鋼鐵巨獸變身公共藝術後，成為新地標。

N

5 頭城車站以北

頭城職人故事展

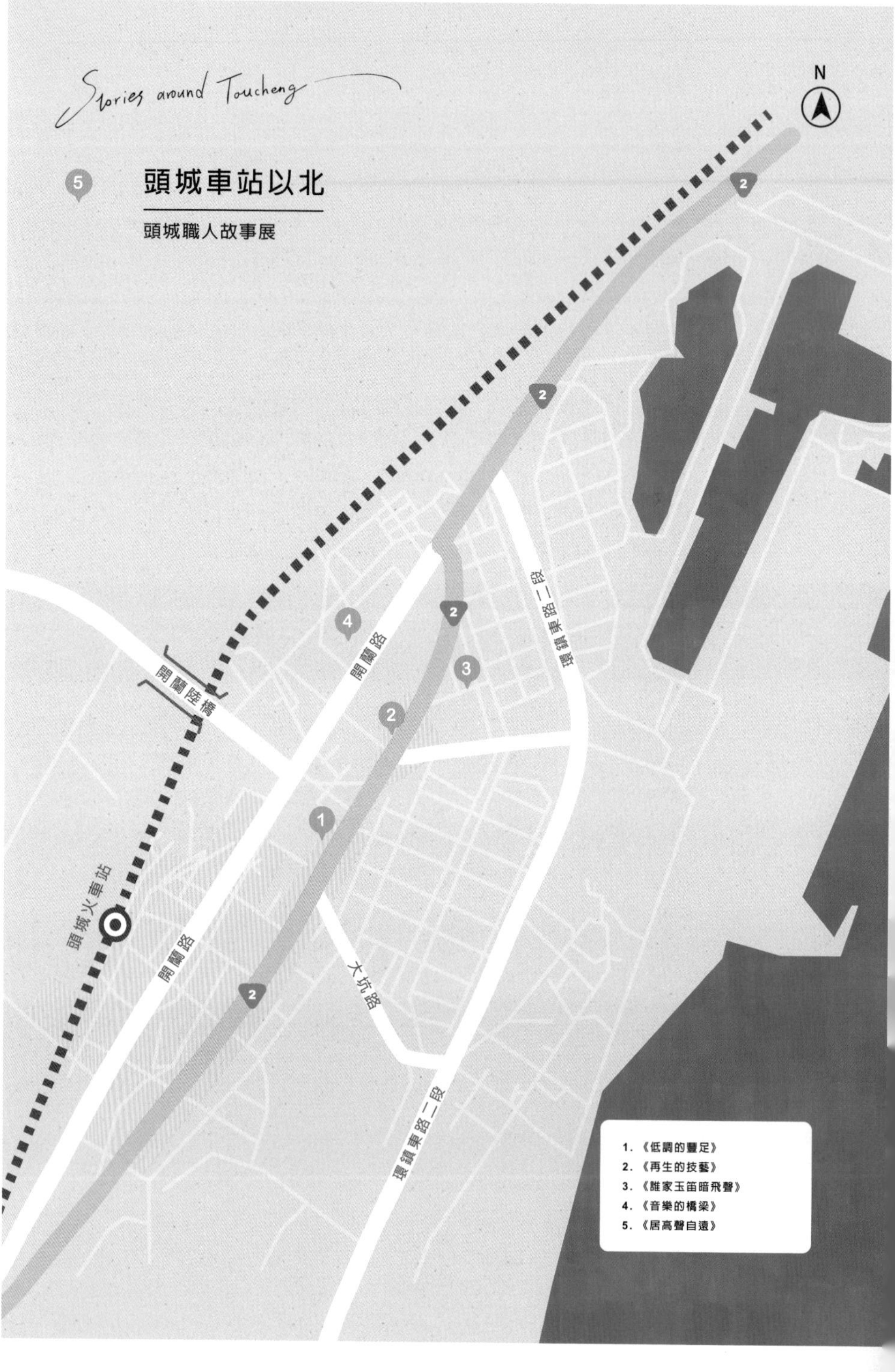

2

2

環頭東路二段

4 開蘭路

2

3

2

開蘭陸橋

1

頭城火車站

開蘭路

2

大坑路

環頭東路二段

1. 《低調的豐足》
2. 《再生的技藝》
3. 《離家玉笛暗飛聲》
4. 《音樂的橋梁》
5. 《居高聲自遠》

車站以北

若以頭城火車站為中心，順省道一路向北，過了
大坑路，視野突然寬廣，職人們就隱身在路旁，
通過小鎮的邊緣呼嘯而去時，不妨感受一下孕育
他們的這個地方。

藝術工藝

低調的豐足

——無師自通木雕師傅・藍文萬

「我頂顢，無愛讀冊……」

「藍文萬木雕工作室」隱身頭城青雲路三段，緊鄰自家經營的檳榔攤，並非現代觀光工廠的窗明几淨。鐵皮屋，懸吊燈泡，地面擺放磨損的電鋸電鑽，電線時而交纏時而錯綜，大小木塊相互堆砌蒙上厚厚灰塵。只允一人容身的空間，彷彿是木雕家對於意志的果斷展現，單純，孤寂，乃至一種值得敬畏的靜默。空氣中，瀰漫淡然的木屑香氣，是檜木，是樟木，是紅豆杉，是牛樟木，是肖楠木，是一整座木質的時光森林。

笑容樸質，言談率直，充滿未經修飾的懇切，眼前這位衣著略顯潦草的男子，便是木雕藝術家藍文萬。幼居貢寮，由於母親宜蘭置產，國二舉家搬遷頭城。年輕時先後學過西點麵包，做過鐵工、臺菜師父，開過小籠包店，曾去三義批發木雕藝品販售，後來放棄生意，回到頭城自學木雕。令人詫異的是，木雕之藝並無求師，全然仰賴長期的摸索、修正與自省。藝術家表示，熟能生巧，必須不斷累積經驗，懂得在錯誤中學習。

「最大的困難，是自己曾經拿著雕刻刀和木

槌，拿了一個鐘頭都沒有動，不知該如何下手。」

所有創作都需要靈感，同時，所有靈感都必須扎根於生活。木雕家的專注凝視，真正體現的，不是虛妄想像，而是對於物的謹慎，對於賦形的敬重，以及對於形與象的重新思索。撿拾漂流木，依照木頭大小，揣測形之可能，再以真實比例相互對照，腦中再三架構，細刀琢磨，人與物相互對望之中，終能逐漸釋出真意。那必須投入大把大把碎銀似的時光，安定心神，淨空所有，讓木雕家與描摹之物，產生精神的內在流動，是以，微觀能視毛蟹纖毛，宏觀能望山川遠景，一切自在於心。

花生、地瓜、蝸牛、蚱蜢、雛雞、金魚、毛蟹、

笑容樸質，充滿未經修飾的懇切，便是木雕藝術家藍文萬給人的印象。

牛隻、柑橘、蒜頭、薑、絲瓜、枯葉、松樹、蒸籠、布袋等，種種素材取自大地隨景，反映三餐食材，以及農家生活最為普遍的日常物件，經由日夜凝視，再次有了親密互動。那是意象的流轉，是神的賦予，更可能是，一位木雕家對於世界萬物，最為堅決的純粹投入。

> 除了經驗累積外，所有創作都需要靈感，所有靈感都必須扎根於生活。

另一方面，我們也從木雕師藍文萬身上，看到實際生活與藝術創作的平衡。「從事藝術的人，也要記得顧腹肚。」話語中，沒有怨嘆，沒有自怨自艾，而是過來人的實際豁達。木雕師叮嚀，**藝術創作者必須尋求肉體與精神的平衡，不能偏廢，同時力求創新，避免故步自封。**

藍文萬木雕師左手持拿雕刻刀，右手持拿木槌，專注凝神，以不同角度凝視眼前尚未完成的木雕，敲打，移動，視其紋路、色澤與曲線，再次進行敲打予以修訂。在這時刻，任何人都不被允許介入，不能輕易驚擾意志的全神貫注。金屬撞擊木頭的聲音陣陣傳來，恍然知曉，那是新生命即將誕生的心跳聲。

1 最初是達摩的作品受人青睞，進而激發他從事木雕的興趣。
2 毛蟹的細緻雕刻為代表性的手法。
3 常以食材等日常物件作為創作內容，雕刻的細微紋路令人讚嘆。

■ ■ ■

Profile

「藍文萬木雕工作室」由木雕、鋼雕藝術創作者創立。
他畢業後曾從事鐵工工作，學得一技之長，同時奠定
了創作的基礎，作品大多取材自過去的生活經驗，雕
出小籠包、毛蟹、田園小雞、蚱蜢等創作。

用手機掃描QR code，深入認識頭城職日生

▲ 收聽訪談　　　▲ 個人簡介

Lan Wen-wan grew up in Gongliao District, New Taipei City, and moved to Toucheng Township, Yilan County, in 8th grade after his mother bought a house there for the

Lan Wen-wan:
Woodcarver & **Owner** of
Lan Wen-wan Woodcarving Studio

family. Before devoting himself to woodcarving, Lan had done various jobs, ranging from pastry-making, metalworking, cooking Chinese cuisine, running a soup dumpling shop, to buying wholesale wood crafts in Sanyi Township, Miaoli County, for resale business. After deciding to return to Toucheng and learn wood carving on his own, he practiced tirelessly—believing that practice makes perfect and that to master a skill, gaining enough experience and learning from one's mistakes are essential. Despite not having a mentor to guide him, he eventually managed to develop exceptional skills through continuous trial and error, refinement, and self-criticism.

Lan noted that every creative endeavor demands a keen eye for detail and a willingness to draw inspiration from life experiences. That is why he makes it a habit to closely observe the objects in his surroundings and constantly seeks to develop a personal bond with them. Drawing inspiration from objects or ingredients commonly found in farming or everyday life, or things that nature has offered to us, such as peanuts, sweet potatoes, snails, grasshoppers, chickens, goldfish, mitten crabs, cows, citrus, garlic, ginger, sponge cucumbers, dead leaves, pine trees, steamers, sacks, etc., he creates remarkable wooden carvings. Through intent observation, contemplation, and determination, he infuses his artworks with personal insights and interpretations.

With a carving chisel in his left hand and a wooden mallet in his right hand, Lan is all focused on the semi-finished wooden carving in front of him, repeatedly examining its patterns, color, and curves from different angles and carving, readjusting, and refining it meticulously. Fully immersed in it, he is unaffected by any outside noise or interruptions. As the sound of a metal chisel and hammer against wood echoes, it is as if "a new life" is about to be born.

再生的技藝

——讓浪板再生・施燦欣

都是因為這片海。衝浪板支撐身體，大海支撐衝浪板，壓低重心站立浪板，維持平衡，伴隨海浪高低起伏。浪至尾端投身入水，再度探出頭時，太陽光正打在海平面，打在曬得黝黑的肌膚，打在任何表層的內在，濕淋淋的大水，散溢片片篩濾的光——**某種層面，我們都是被大海收回洗淨的子民。**

施燦欣，暱稱李小龍，原就讀光電系，大三開始至頭城衝浪，受到衝浪文化強烈吸引，人生彷彿自此轉了一個彎，從陸地踏上大海兩棲度日。從大四開始，臺北宜蘭兩地遷。最初在番薯衝浪店打工，後向阿頭（A Toh）師傅學習修復浪板，擔任學徒兩年。畢業退伍，正式遷居頭城。剛開始的學徒收入，無法支撐生活，輾轉任職雪隧消防隊，而後再由師傅阿頭手上承繼「板再生專業浪板維修」。

「板再生」接鄰頭城國小，所在據點「衝浪公賣局」原為頭城菸酒公賣局，承租之後，2022年6月正式創立複合式工作室，可說是一個小型的衝浪聚落。一樓分為兩區，前方為「VAST費雪奇普仕 FISH & CHIPS 澳洲炸魚薯條」，後方為「板再生」。二樓則分為三區，包含創辦

人阿頭 ATOHA SURFBOARDS 手工衝浪板製作、
Aloha 椰殼碗工作室和 Ohjet1 藝術工作室。複合工
作室能夠成立，都是因為參與其中的成員，相當熱
愛衝浪，想要積極推動衝浪教育；當然，再往內探，
則是對於海洋文化的喜愛。由最初的衝浪活動，深
入理解，廣泛推廣，進而聚集一群志同道合者齊心

施燦新除了讓浪板再
生外，更希望推廣衝
浪文化。

協力，為了「Surf City」的理念，默默努力。

浪板受損，如同人體受傷。修復過程相當繁瑣，過程約可分為清創、填縫、打磨、塑形、包覆玻璃纖維、打磨、樹脂塗層、打磨、拋光等步驟，每一步驟都得搭配不同器具，必須細心面對，耐心處置，不可操之過急。要成為一位合格的補板師，須得歷經三年以上的培訓養成。此外，過程之中，打磨會產生大量粉塵，噴漆會沾染顏料，夏日則得滿頭大汗忍受酷熱，工作絲毫不輕鬆，願意以此為志業者並不多。如今每個月，約可收到一百張左右的板修復，整體運作已上軌道。

> 成員們熱愛衝浪，想積極推動衝浪教育；論其初衷，則是對於海洋文化的喜愛。

衝浪文化當然需要培養，而且必須從孩童開始培養。臺灣鄰海，卻是懼水之島，由於政經歷史背景，大海向來不予向民眾開放，導致多年內向陸棲。從認識衝浪文化作為起始，乘風破浪，期待觀念漸次鬆綁，大幅拉近民眾對於大海的距離。施燦欣表示，除了衝浪板修復之外，衝浪公賣局的團隊還會不定期舉辦各項活動，包含浪況分享會、削板師分享座談、繪畫教學、二手衝浪交流 x 起秋市集、浪

| | 2 |
|1| 3 |

1 複合式的工作室中，結合許多夥伴一起工作。
2 浪板修復過程相當繁瑣，需要有相當的耐心與細心。
3 修復中的浪板。

板交換贈公益活動等。此外，除了早先就已設立的工作室外，更預計改建店址外側空地，從停車場改建為滑板場，力圖推廣「衝浪滑板」新式運動。

　　浪板的再生，複合工作室的相互支援，我們在施燦欣以及共同匯聚的浪人身上，看到的是一片遼闊的海——日夜響起濤聲，卻又靜靜等待我們的日常涉入。

...

Profile

板再生由阿頭（A Toh）創立，施燦欣學藝後，繼承「板再生專業浪板維修」，除為衝浪者服務外，更希望藉此基地聚集志同道合者，推廣衝浪文化，構築「Surf City」。

用手機掃描QR code，深入認識頭城職日生

▲收聽訪談　　　▲臉書粉專

Shi Can-xin, nicknamed Bruce Lee, first tried surfing in Toucheng when he was a junior in college and soon fell in love with it and the surfing culture. He went on to work part-time at Surffella, a surf shop in Toucheng, and then apprenticed under Master A Toh

Shi Can-xin:
Surfboard-Repair Expert

for two years, learning how to repair surfboards. After graduating from college and completing his military service, he moved to Toucheng and continued his apprenticeship, while also working for the Hsuehshan Tunnel Fire Department to support himself. After acquiring the necessary skills, he inherited his master's surfboard repair workshop—Surfboards Reborn.

Shi noted that a damaged surfboard is like an injured human body. The repair process is quite complicated, and each step must be approached with care and patience. Rushing the process is not advisable. To become a qualified surfboard repair technician, one must undergo training for at least three years. Nowadays, the workshop receives around 100 repair orders per month, and the overall operation has been running smoothly.

Surfboards Reborn is currently located in a composite surfboard workshop called "Surfing Monopoly," which he established in June 2022 on the site of the former Taiwan Tobacco and Wine Monopoly Bureau, next to Toucheng Elementary School. Surfing Monopoly can be regarded as a small surfing "community," as it not only creates and repairs surfboards but also provides American-style snacks.

Shi pointed out that Taiwan is surrounded by the sea, but due to its political and economic historical background, the sea has never been fully accessible to the public, leading to many people being less close to the ocean or even fearing it. He hopes that through this composite workshop, more people can get to know and fall in love with surfing and then influence those around them to change this established impression of the ocean. At the same time, he hopes to gather more and more like-minded people to work together and create a "Surf City."

From Shi and his working partners, we can see a great passion for surfing, a love for the sea, and a spirit of mutual assistance. Working in unison, they share a common goal: to attract more people to Toucheng and make surfing a part of their daily lives.

誰家玉笛暗飛聲

文化教育

——音樂的傳播・董幸霖

玉笛悠悠吹奏，二胡款款拉弦，我們停下腳步側耳傾聽。

董幸霖，1991 年生，頭城囡仔。就讀臺灣藝術大學國樂系期間，主修二胡，副修鋼琴，大二開始學習樂團指揮，現為頭城國小國樂團、佛光大學國樂社及宜蘭多所學校國樂指導老師。2014 年成立二胡個人工作室，逐漸積累教學經驗；2017 年成立「頭圍堡藝術工作室」，擔任創意總監，積極參與頭城、礁溪等地的區域性表演，如歷年的街頭音樂會、慈善音樂會和史雲湖音樂會等。2021 和 2022 年由於受到新冠疫情影響，暫時停止展演，然而工作室仍然逆風挺立，重心回歸教學。

頭圍堡藝術工作室位於頭城國小東側，越過青雲路三段，可見一排三層樓連棟住宅，最右側即是乾淨明亮的工作室。一、二樓為工作室，三樓自用，整體空間採複合式設計。左右兩側為大片落地透明櫥窗，入門之後，中間是一長形木屋，可供學生、朋友與藝術人士談詩論藝；右側陳列各式樂器，包含二胡、高胡與竹笛等；後

側是簡易吧檯，供予茶水；左側為獨立空間，擺設平台鋼琴，且可作為一對一中、小型樂器教學。二樓打造寬敞空間，除了擺放另一平台鋼琴，尚可容納數十人，平時可用作團體班級授課、大型樂器多人練習，以及權充中型表演場地。

　　董幸霖表示，除了保留教室進行教學，更希望整體空間能夠輕鬆自在，不必有嚴肅、制式與刻意的感覺，**希望音樂自然而然融入生活，而非束之高閣，或作為浮華裝飾。**

　　「我出生在這個地方，在這個地方長大，受到很多人的恩惠。」董幸霖開設頭圍堡藝術工作室的主要原因，便是希望能夠以最短的距離、最低的費用，

成立頭圍堡藝術工作室是為了讓頭城人有更親近的音樂教育場所。

供予頭城子弟有一個學習音樂的舒適空間。音樂教室如同種子，將會逐漸成長茁壯，蔚為風景。如今約有 20 多位學員，定期來到工作室進行個別訓練，包含幼稚園學子、成人和退休人士不等。

> 希望音樂能輕鬆自在，不必有嚴肅、制式與刻意，自然而然融入生活。

任何一門藝術的推廣，洵是充滿挑戰。董幸霖展望未來，除了持續向下扎根，更希望藉由不同型態的演繹，能有藝術跨域的結合、創新與共創；此外，亦不排斥舉辦快閃音樂會，或者在著名地標特殊場域進行演出。嘗試的目的，無非**希望能夠以迥然不同、別具匠心的表演形式，持續帶動在地藝文產業**。董幸霖最大的心願，就是期望透過自己小小的努力，讓頭城鎮上洋溢不同的藝術文化——流行之音古典之樂，東方之譜西方之曲，藝術的交響合奏，足以形成集體的複音共鳴。

「我這個時候不回來，我要等到什麼時候？」

董幸霖沒有惶惑，不曾遲疑，樂器是情

1	3
2	

1 期望透過自己小小的努力，讓頭城鎮上洋溢不同的藝術文化。
2 工作室也可成為團練空間。（圖片提供：董幸霖）
3 二胡、高胡與竹笛等樂器展示陳列。

感的表達,是交流的媒介,是精神的暫時安棲。彈奏鋼琴,吹響竹笛,持弓推拉二胡,情緒或飽滿或留白,他將自己的身體、行動與精神,化為故鄉的樂器,撥彈吹奏之中,時刻發出最為深刻的動人聲音。

Profile

頭圍堡藝術工作室由董幸霖於 2017 年成立,為專業的音樂工作室,提供音樂課程規劃、教學及藝文演出。用音樂記錄這片土地,希望以最近的距離、最低的費用,提供頭城子弟學習音樂的舒適空間。

用手機掃描QR code,深入認識頭城職日生

▲ 收聽訪談

▲ Instagram

Dung Xin-lin, a native of Toucheng, is currently teaching in several schools' Chinese music clubs in Yilan, including Toucheng Elementary School and Fo Guang University.

Dung Xin-lin:
Creative Director of
Touweibao Art Studio

He went to the National Taiwan University of Arts to study Chinese music, majoring in erhu and minoring in piano. He also started learning orchestra conducting in his sophomore year. In 2014, he established his own erhu studio, gradually gaining teaching experience. In 2017, he founded the Touweibao Art Studio, a music studio offering various instrument courses, and served as the creative director. Throughout the years, he has been actively participating in local music performances, street music concerts, and benefit concerts in Toucheng and Jiaoxi, such as the Shi Yun Lake Concert. Although he was unable to perform in 2021 and 2022 due to COVID-19, he remained actively involved in the Chinese music industry by dedicating himself to teaching music at the studio.

"I was born and raised here, and I have received a lot of help from many people." With the intention to give back to the community, Dung founded the Touweibao Art Studio, hoping to provide a comfortable music instrument learning space for locals to learn an instrument with minimum commuting time and expenses. He believes that the music studio will grow and thrive gradually, just like a seed, which will bring about positive changes to the local community over time. Today, the studio has more than 20 students from a diverse range of age groups, including kindergarten children, adults, and retirees. They come to the studio regularly and are given customized music instruction that suits their individual needs.

His greatest wish is that one day his hometown can be a place where different arts and music—be it pop or classical music, Eastern or Western music—can coexist in perfect harmony, creating an enchanting artistic ambiance; he earnestly hopes that he can play a small but significant role in it.

音樂的橋梁

——從阿根廷到頭城的音樂家‧明馬丁

　　Musa，來自阿根廷布宜諾斯艾利斯省，一位鋼琴家，一位鍵琴手，同時身兼作曲、編曲、歌曲製作人等職，時常在不同樂團之中擔任團長或重要角色。中文名字明馬丁，是在臺灣簽訂結婚證書時所定，「明」是為了紀念祖父 Mingo 而取的姓氏。同多位知名音樂藝人合作，曾經入圍金曲獎，獲得金音獎諸多獎項，是國內流行音樂界享有高知名度的音樂創作者。

　　舞臺演出的足跡遍及世界，爾後遷居臺灣，落腳宜蘭頭城。在金魚厝邊的鼎力協助之下，2022 年 3 月以高級專業人才身分，正式取得中華民國國民身分。

　　「臺灣是一個很特別的地方，因為有很多矛盾。臺灣人很有禮貌，跟日本差不多，太多禮貌會造成冷漠，但是臺灣卻很熱情。」在明馬丁眼中，臺灣是一充滿矛盾的禮儀之邦，不似日本人拘謹，不似熱帶國家狂躁，巧妙平衡於冷靜與熱情之間。

　　明馬丁指出，**來到臺灣，剛開始所有東西都是新的**，必須用手去指，用耳去聽，用嘴唇發出異國聲音，不斷摸索學習。毫無預設的情況下，產生彈性，不會因為現實與預期的落差而感挫折。臺灣有其獨特，例如擁有堪稱全世界最優良的捷運，擁有

明馬丁目前可以用簡單的中文表達想法。

世界級晶圓代工龍頭公司台積電（TSMC），一個小小的島嶼竟能孕育各種不同的氣候與風景。

「頭城對我而言，是一個小的臺灣。」定居於此，是因為這裡有山有海空氣好，能看見天空，能曬到太陽，週間人群少，生活機能相當齊全。若有閒暇，騎著腳踏車便能四處蹓躂。住處遠離都市，擁有不受限制的創作空間，還能在日常生活之中獲得靈感，一方面保有私隱，一方面隨時能夠向外開展。小鎮交通便利，無論是工作演奏或學校授課，搭乘大眾交通運輸即可前往臺北。

對於明馬丁而言，頭城是一處可進可退宜室宜家的安居之地。

「我沒有一個音樂風格。」拒絕單一風格，是最為強烈的風格。明馬丁以簡單的中文表達想法，穿插英文與西班牙文，動用靈活的手勢與豐富的肢體動作加以補充，三種語言不斷流動，此種自覺與不自覺的跨越，具

體反映於音樂創作。第一張專輯是爵士樂，第二張專輯融合北美洲、南美洲和亞洲各地曲風，第三張專輯是拉丁 Live，第四張專輯是電子樂，優哉游哉穿梭其中，風格不斷突破，實踐個體精神。明馬丁的音樂，根植自我經驗，戮力跨越，具有吸納、交融與涵養的特性。

> 頭城有山有海空氣好，能看見天空，曬到太陽，是生活機能相當齊全的安居之地。

「我想要知道在沒有標籤的情況下，自己的音樂生涯能夠走得多遠。」

不管走得多遠，終究得回返自我。音樂的哲學，很大一部分便是透過聲音表達自己。想要產生與眾不同的音樂風格，必須先相信自己，由此激發內在的生命力。明馬丁點出當代音樂，時常因為商業操作盲目模仿，迷失了方向。所謂自己，務必向內觀看，杜絕盲目跟隨，並從個體探入集體的文化、命運與歷史。

「了解自己是非常重要的，需要讓你的靈魂平平安安，如果你的靈魂亂七八糟，那就沒有辦法了。」

移動者的遷居，往往擁有多元的開放關係，扎根日常，將所在視為基地，同時有效打破地域疆界，持續向外擴展。

明馬丁藉由音樂所揭示的，乃是精神的錨定、接軌與串聯，如同一座橋梁。定居頭城以來，曾有不少音樂

創作者慕名前來，尋求合作；此外，多次參與頭城老街文化藝術季，同在地與國際藝術家進行合作。

2021 年 3 月，為了慶祝國際婦女節，阿根廷商務文化辦事處擇定金魚厝邊，以「『向女性致敬：一段血淚斑斑的歷史』指尖上心的悸動」為題，展示兩位畫家作品：定居頭城的阿根廷藝術家明蓮花（明馬丁之妻），以及旅居阿根廷的臺灣藝術家周欣璇。同時，邀請明馬丁於開幕現場演奏。阿根廷商務文化辦事處處長韋修索（Director Miguel Alfredo Velloso）及其夫人，特別蒞臨參與活動。2022 年 12 月，明馬丁則以新臺灣人的身分受邀，帶領樂團前往印度，參與印度理工學院孟買分校（IIT Bombay）一年一度的 Mood Indigo 文化節。

無可諱言，明馬丁以自身的創作，展現一股超越族群、文化與意識形態的力量，除了藉由音樂完成自我，更彰顯在地與國際的對位和鳴。

定居頭城取得中華民國身分後，讓藝術家可以留在臺灣專心發展。

Profile

來自阿根廷布宜諾斯艾利斯的明馬丁，是國際音樂人，目前定居頭城，不但與張惠妹、曹格、盧廣仲、王若琳、MATZKA、阿爆等知名音樂藝人合作，並曾經入圍金曲獎，獲得金音獎諸多獎項。

用手機掃描QR code，深入認識頭城職日生

▲收聽訪談

▲臉書粉專

Musa (Martin Musaubach), now living in Taiwan, is a renowned musician from Argentina who works as a pianist, keyboard player, composer, arranger, music producer, etc.

Musa:
Renowned Musician and Founder of 3690 Studios LTDA

Having cooperated with many famous music artists, been nominated for the Golden Melody Award, and won awards such as the Golden Indie Music Award, Musa has enjoyed great fame in the pop music community in Taiwan.

Before moving to Taiwan, Musa had performed in many different parts of the world. In March 2022, he became a naturalized citizen in Taiwan, approved under the high-level professional program. He resides in Toucheng because it is a town with mountains and the sea, clean air, and easy access to Taipei, allowing him to be away from the

hustle and bustle of city living, protect his privacy, create freely, and draw inspiration from daily life—all while remaining connected to the outside world.

"I am curious to know how far I can go in my music career when I am not labeled as anything."

Musa believes that music is largely about self-expression and that if you want to have a unique music style or unleash your inner creative potential, you have to believe in yourself first.

Musa expresses himself well through his music creations, and his music seems to possess the power that can break through ethnic, cultural, and ideological boundaries. Ever since he settled in Toucheng, he has participated in the Toucheng Old Street Arts and Culture Festival multiple times and collaborated with various local and international artists. He has attracted numerous music artists to come to Toucheng, helping to bridge the local community of Toucheng and the international community.

From him, we see resilience and confidence shine from within. With an unrelenting passion, he persists in using music as a medium to explore life and express himself, sharing his happiness and sadness, as well as all other feelings that words cannot convey.

居高聲自遠──打造無為而治的山林·石正人

公眾環境

　　山路向前，樹木繁茂綠意蜿蜒不止，日子帶有氤氳水霧，總在一個轉角之後，發現前方有路。「蜻蜓石」是山間民宿，海拔 250 公尺，占地 13 公頃，倚靠雪山山脈北側，居高臨下，遠眺龜山島，俯瞰蘭陽平原，太平洋盡在眼前。群山庇護，無車馬喧，自然萬物都在幽靜之中發出各自的聲音，是風，是落雨，是雞鳴，是藍鵲啼叫，是枝幹斷裂的聲音，沒有被刻意美化，沒有被過度開墾，適切回歸人與自然最初的樣貌。

　　石正人，1956 年生，苗栗苑裡人，臺大昆蟲系名譽教授，現已退休，專心打理民宿。2000 年在頭城購買原始山坡地，以生態工法整地，砍草移樹，清出一小塊土地種菜，逐漸擴大區域，嘗試在開墾與環境保育之中取得平衡。8 年整地，3 年蓋房，直到 2011 年才完成建築主體。民宿的命名，是因原址有一水池，雨後時常聚集蜻蜓；此外建物本身，亦以蜻蜓作為主體造型。

　　蜻蜓石最引人矚目的，是石正人以自身的專業，躬身實踐環境教育，並且孕育人類與自然互相依賴、尊重與互惠的生存倫理。土地僅只利用 5 公頃，其他地區保留為自然保護區，設有 6 條步道可供漫遊。民宿居中，下方設立層層梯田，種植蔬菜，

石正人希望能在頭城終老一生，真正融入山上的自然環境。

是政府正式驗證的有機農場；上方搭建溫室育苗，搭設棚舍飼雞、養黑水虻。梯田所植的有機菜蔬，包含白菜、芥菜、青江菜、空心菜、青蔥、蘿蔔嬰、萵苣、高麗菜、香菜等，水果有香蕉、金棗、火龍果、木瓜等。

山上可取得約 70% 食材，民宿一切吃食，採以自然生態循環系統。種植有機蔬菜，不施化肥，廚餘用來飼養黑水虻，黑水虻犀雜飼料養雞，雞可生蛋，雞肉和雞蛋再回到餐桌。此外，養蜂可替蔬果授粉，同時產生蜂蜜。至於雞和蟲產生的糞便，用來堆肥滋養蔬果。整體而言，意圖建立一個相互仰

賴的共生系統，讓自然界維持平衡，既競爭又合作，看似放生卻又相互制約──只要給予足夠時間，便能如老子思想般無為而治。

以生態工法整地，嘗試在開墾與環境保育之中取得平衡，歷經 11 年才有建築主體。

「人類應該要回歸自然。」石正人表示，每一位訪客，無論大小，都會由他親自授課約 40 分鐘，講述農場特色、有機農業和循環生態，接續是一個半到兩個小時的現場導覽，希望透過訪客的切身臨場，加強人與自然的連結，進而推廣環境教育。「幾千萬年來的演化，才有現今的各個物種，現在卻有可能一夕絕種，這是危機。」

此外，新穎的民宿建物，擺放的卻是古董家具，這正是對於物的再次利用。這些曾經被使用過的家具，傳遞的不是人類無止無盡的需求，而是溫潤的歷史感，彷彿贖回年代，藉此重新思索，器物在人類文明所存有的功能、位置與記憶。

「我希望未來能在頭城終老一生，真正融入山上的自然環境。」石正人面向蘭陽平原，望向大海，露出童真似的微笑，那是真正踩踏

| 1 | 3 |
| 2 | 4 |

1 從空中鳥瞰蜻蜓石建築，像一隻停駐在山谷中的蜻蜓。
2 蜻蜓石所在可見平原與海灣。
3 挑高的大廳，視野寬闊。
3 民宿七成食材都有機且能自給自足。

泥土的人，才能擁有的爽朗面容。

居高聲自遠，我們側耳所聽，正是雨後蜻蜓快速展翅的聲音。

■■■

Profile

由昆蟲學者石正人和 Jessie 一手打造的蜻蜓石民宿，坐靠雪山山脈出海口，鳥瞰宜蘭灣全景。山上原本有一座水池，蜻蜓漫天飛舞，所以房子師法蜻蜓，蓋個像蜻蜓的造型，蜻蜓石就這樣誕生了！

用手機掃描QR code，深入認識頭城職日生

▲收聽訪談　　▲臉書粉專

Shih Cheng-jen grew up in Yuanli Township, Miaoli County, and later became a professor of entomology at National Taiwan University. After retiring as an emeritus professor, he got into the business of running a B&B. In

Shih Cheng-jen:
Founder of Stonbo Lodge

2000, he bought a piece of undeveloped mountain land in Toucheng Township, Yilan County, and used eco-friendly land clearing techniques to uproot and clear vegetation, preparing the land for construction. He also cleared a small section of land for vegetable cultivation and gradually expanded the area, seeking to strike a balance between development and environmental conservation. After eight years of land preparation and another three years of construction, the main structure of the lodge, bearing resemblance to a dragonfly, was completed in 2011.

Shih named it "Stonbo Lodge," combining the English word "Stone" (which has the same meaning as his Chinese surname) and the Japanese word for dragonfly "Tonbo." The most distinctive aspect of this lodge is that "environmental sustainability" is at the core of its design. Shih drew on his ecological knowledge to create a space that embodies the mutually beneficial relationship between humans and nature. Only five hectares of land was used for development, with the remaining area carefully designated as a nature reserve, featuring six trails for visitors to wander through.

According to Shih, about 70% of ingredients can be obtained on the mountain, allowing him to produce and provide food for the guests in a way that aligns with sustainable principles. He grows organic vegetables without using chemical fertilizers, makes them into food, feeds leftovers to black soldier flies, and mixes them with other feed to raise chickens that produce eggs and meat—both of which can later be made into food. In addition, he keeps bees for pollination and their honey and uses chicken and worm manure as compost to help vegetables and fruits grow. He hopes that through these efforts, a virtuous and sustainable ecological cycle can be formed, gradually reaching a state of balance in nature—much like the state of perfect equilibrium intended in Lao Tzu's philosophy of "Wu Wei" (the art of "doing nothing").

"I hope to spend the rest of my life in Toucheng, fully immersing myself in the natural environment of this mountain," said Shih, facing the Lanyang Plain and the Pacific Ocean with a childlike smile on his face—the kind of cheerful expression that only someone who has worked assiduously in nature with an unwavering love for it can have.

Come and visit the natural wonders in Toucheng. Rain or shine, breathtaking scenery awaits, along with enchanting sounds of nature, such as the wing-fluttering sound of dragonflies flying by.

蜿蜒山林裡的產業步道

帶路人
講故事

林志全

微笑灣農場主人，曾經是頭城、中華國中校長，提前退休後將山上果園打造成休閒農場。

頭城蘭陽技術學院後方，長長的石階通往神聖的處所。

沿著鄉間小路，穿過田野，兩側有農田、潺潺的小水圳、一畦畦的水田，淺水清澈，清涼的微風吹過，清晨的陽光和煦溫暖，鄰旁的青山與天空的白雲倒映在水面上，沿著石階蜿蜒而上，我們來到頭城大修宮，當地人俗稱「仙公廟」，主祀孚佑帝君（呂洞賓），創建於民國 39 年（西元 1950 年），神聖而莊嚴的廟宇，同時也是平時踏青的好去處，廟前寬闊的廣場可以眺望龜山島與頭城一帶的平野田疇及海岸風光，視野遼闊，展望極佳。

從山下前往廟的路上，時不時能看見一些零星的橘子還在樹上。過去，橘子曾是頭城賣往日本的高價經濟作物之一，當時漫山遍野的橘子樹，豐年時果園結實纍纍，換來的是一戶戶人家不愁吃穿的幸福笑容。經過時不妨停下來，享受

微風徐徐，回味這段古老的歷史。

　　大修宮附近坐落著北門坑福德廟，福德廟面對著北門坑溪，廟的右前方有一小片蓮霧林，這裡早期出產番石榴，後來則廣泛種植蓮霧，蓮霧也曾經是此地農產品的大宗。儘管古道早已失去交通功能，但大修宮步道仍是踏青健行路線的好去處，假日時可以來此感受大自然的美好。（口述／林志全，文字／楊宇伶）

■ ■ ■

1. 林志全覺得郊山適合健行，遠眺平原海岸讓人心曠神怡。**2.** 產業道路適合步行，沿路還可一探祕境。
3. 沿路樹上的果實，提醒這裡曾經是繁茂的果園。**4.** 大修宮在柳暗花明之處，是當地人的私房景點。

Stories around Toucheng

頭城五漁村
頭城職人故事展

石城火車站

大里火車站

大溪火車站

龜山火車站

外澳火車站

N

1. 《言說不盡》
2. 《我們在這裡生活》
3. 《海上的木質森林》
4. 《歸去來兮》
5. 《在海上》
6. 《大海的贈予》

五漁村

Toucheng Old Street

頭城緊鄰著海，五漁村像接縫上的明珠閃耀。
海上有鯨豚；漁港邊、社區裡有著先人的生活
足跡；節慶時搶孤熱鬧、北管高亢，嘗一嘗海
產是必要。

在地產業

言說不盡

——深入社區再生家鄉・劉厚漢

烏石漁港，我們將從這裡出發。

太平洋就在眼前，龜山島矗立大海遠近守護，遠遊者歸返，拜訪者探尋，戍守者仰起頭顱追述歷史，有些湮沒的故事，有些消散的浪紋，有些隱藏的礦脈，必須用時日來換。表達是確認，介紹為組構，運用聲音傳遞力量，將見證的一切細膩轉譯，說自己的生命，談區域的變革，藉由當下言及地方的往昔與未來。

滔滔之言，正是對於故鄉彌久不渝的熱愛。

劉厚漢，1959 年生，頭城更新里人。父為果農，專植砂糖橘，從小隨父遍行宜蘭，探查土質、水文與氣候。高中畢業，短暫從事水電，1980 年代進入公務部門，1990 年代從事社區營造工作，2005 年正式加入賞鯨行業，展開地方導覽，現擔任宜蘭縣體育會理事長、更新社區發展協會總幹事與宜蘭縣觀光大使協進會理事等職。

提到頭城早期的社區營造工作，必須提及劉厚漢。1990 年代，臺灣內部展開思辨，意欲重新定義在地文化，「社區總體

1990 年代劉厚漢就參與社區營造工作。

營造」應運而生，社區發展工作交付民間主導，政府正式退位從旁協助。劉厚漢以合興社區（位於頭城鎮合興里）總幹事身分，秉持永續經營的理念，凝聚社區意識，再以硬體設施搭配自然環境形塑在地，使合興社區一舉獲得全國富麗漁村冠軍、全省綠美化績優社區等榮耀。對於在地，劉厚漢並不直截橫植理論，而是扎扎實實理解地方風情、人文歷史與自然環境，由此重新展開定位。

「必須要深入社區。」數十年來，專注濱海漁村的再生營造，義無反顧投入導覽工作。

對於劉厚漢而言，**社區營造與導覽解說實為一體兩面**。所有蘊含意義的探入，都需要在地人的聲

音、眼光與視野，為我們詳細釋義。來到濱海五漁村 (石城、大里、大溪、梗枋及外澳)，必須述說定置漁網、大船出港、移民遷居、淡蘭古道與礁岩環境；來到開蘭頭城，必須述說吳沙入蘭、頭圍港今昔、老街繁華與特色農產；

秉持永續理念，凝聚社區意識，理解地方風情、人文歷史與自然後，再展開定位。

來到乘風破浪的賞鯨船，必須述說蘭博設計、龜山八景、蘭陽八景、黑潮暖流、鯨豚保育、漁業生態與烏石港歷史等。小至物件，大至年代，眼前見聞，誠是故鄉一切——得仔細聽，得認真說，得好好感受山海的和鳴共奏。

「你看到了什麼？」劉厚漢拋出疑問。

身處其中，往往看見卻又視而不見，需要一次一次善意提醒。

「老天爺給我們的有限資源，要做合理的、適度的保育，讓人類永續使用，我們的生活才會幸福。」劉厚漢次次提及，臺灣只有海洋事業，沒有海洋文化，不斷進行資源的消耗、奪取與濫用，若沒有積極建立生態保育觀念，無疑將會導致未來的災難。從最初的社區營造，

1	
	3
2	

1 數十年來，專注濱海漁村的再生營造，義無反顧投入導覽工作。（圖片提供：劉厚漢）

2 對劉厚漢而言，社區營造與導覽解說實為一體兩面。（圖片提供：劉厚漢）

3 劉厚漢加入賞鯨行業與生態導覽，讓更多人感受永續的重要性。（圖片提供：劉厚漢）

到生態導覽、鯨豚介紹、蘭陽歷史探查，再到對於海洋的保護倡議，劉厚漢持之以恆，不倦不怠，為了故鄉再三喉舌——那早已超過單純口述，而是發自內心的真摯情感。

　　言說不盡，不曾窮盡，因為留待接續的，總有自己未盡的故事。

Profile

擔任過更新社區發展協會總幹事，曾從事水電工程工作，後來進入頭城鎮公所服務，負責路燈維護相關事務。2005 年涉入賞鯨旅遊業，促成新港澳休閒農漁業發展協會成立，希望分享在地資源，進而帶動當地農漁業者發展觀光旅遊產業。

用手機掃描QR code，深入認識頭城職日生

▲收聽訪談　　▲合興社區

Liu Hou-han is a native of Gengxin District, Toucheng. His father, a fruit farmer specializing in growing tangerines, had taken him around Yilan to investigate the soil quality, hydrology, and climatic conditions of various

Liu Hou-han: Promoter of Community Development and Environmental Sustainability

places since he was a child. After graduating from high school, he briefly worked as a plumber and an electrician. In the 1980s, he joined the public sector, and in the 1990s, he worked on community development projects. In 2005, he decided to dedicate himself to the whale-watching tourist industry and began offering local guided tours.

There was a trend in Taiwan in the 1990s to redefine "local culture," which later gave rise to the concept of community development. Back then, Liu was the executive secretary of the Hexing Community Development Association (located in Hexing Village, Toucheng Township). He rallied the community and, in response to the government's fishing village policy, promoted the establishment of Hexing Fishing Village. Featuring sustainable designs and physical structures that blend harmoniously with the natural environment and show distinctive local characteristics, Hexing Fishing Village has been recognized by the government as a model village and has been selected as one of the top-performing communities for its green beautification efforts.

"Deep involvement with the community is very important." For decades, Liu has been actively promoting the revitalization and reconstruction of coastal fishing villages and engaging in tour guiding. He believes that community development and tour guiding are closely intertwined. To truly get to know a community, it is crucial to know the perspectives and insights of the locals and listen to what they have to say.

"God has blessed us with limited resources, and we should use them in a reasonable, appropriate, and conservative way to ensure the sustainable use of resources and the well-being of all people," said Liu. He mentioned several times that people in Taiwan tended to only care about the development of the marine industry, not paying much attention to marine culture and resource conservation. However, as he pointed out, continuously consuming, exploiting, and overusing resources would lead to disastrous consequences in the future.

To safeguard the ecological environment and cultural heritage of his hometown, Liu has consistently dedicated himself to relevant conservation and advocacy efforts. By actively engaging in conducting ecological tours, introducing people to dolphins and whales, investigating Yilan's history, advocating marine protection, and more, he has made significant and meaningful contributions towards this cause—out of his deep love for his hometown.

文化教育

我們在這裡生活
—— 為港口社區提供全方位服務・吳季信、吳誌祥

這不是一個人的故事，而是一個社區團隊相互支援的故事。

吳季信，1955 年生，原先從事建築業，退休之後由地方鄉親推薦，擔任港口社區理事長。身為一位社區領導，吳季信展現的不是長袖善舞，不是華麗詞藻，不是模糊遠景，而是一種唯有根植在地，才能適切養成的草根、務實與積極行動力。**事務不假他人，必先躬身，替港口社區提供全方位服務。**

2022 年 10 月，頭城鎮港口社區發展協會在「機槍堡遺址公園 (110 年新成立，位於港口海堤步道南岸)」的大草坪，展示在地悠久文化「肉粽棧」——那是一個以搶孤孤棧為原型，縮小版本的公共裝置藝術。頭城搶孤遠近馳名，是臺灣最為重要的民俗慶典之一，原初舉辦目的，是為紀念先民橫渡黑水溝艱辛移墾。漢人遷居拓荒，必然歷經天災、瘴癘、惡疾與族群齟齬等考驗，逝者不知所終，無處可歸，成為孤魂野鬼。頭城居民舉辦搶孤，以祀先人，表達後人深遠的追念敬重。從最初的超渡施食，賑濟孤苦，演變為團隊競技，最後轉型為結合體育、民俗、觀光與文化演繹的代表性活動。

農曆七月搶孤，鄉里熱切參與，有別其他鄰里採用的魷魚、米粉、鴨賞、臘肉等真空包裝供品，

港口里的孤棧為「肉粽棧」，非假他人之手，非視便利，由村民自行備料紮粽，製程繁複，費時費工。糯米得炒熟，包裹蝦仁、香菇等內餡，再予冷凍，一千多顆肉粽必須動員村內大大小小才得以完成。吳季信娓娓道來，包含孤棧刺竹的原料取得、製作過程、運輸方式、相關禁忌，以及搶孤步行運送孤棧的流程等，感慨表示，如今，熟稔這項民俗技藝的耆老日漸凋零，已不超過十人。

　　港口社區活動中心前設立一祈福棧，機槍堡遺址公園則有三根縮小版肉粽棧，突破禁忌，以公共藝術形式展現，期待社會大眾對於搶孤文化有更深的認識。

吳季信（左）、吳誌祥（中）替港口社區提供全方位服務。

此外，吳寄信亦對社區發展不遺餘力。耆老經驗無法輕易取代，那都是來自生命的不斷累積，才能收穫熟成，包含綁孤棧的獨門技術、牽罟、農作物種植經驗、在地特色食物烹調，以及各種生活器物如漁網、畚箕、竹簍等的修補製作。如果沒有妥善傳承，設法留下珍貴的庶民文化，一旦耆老逝去，過往的技藝與記憶將不復存在。

> 有別其他鄰里，港口里的孤棧為「肉粽棧」，須動員全村一同備料紮粽。

吳誌祥，1989 年生，暱稱小黑。原先從事老人長照服務多年，後來得知小鎮人口老齡化嚴峻，亟需青年挹注，106 年回到土生土長的濱海社區進行服務，發揮所長。這當然是幸運且幸福的事——小鎮所能提供的工作，多屬初階的服務或勞務，例如餐飲、工地或是家族經營的小店。學有專精的青年為了尋求更好發展，必然外移，即使願意待在成長故鄉，卻無相應職缺，人口老化的情況遂日漸嚴重。

憑恃一己之力面對長者，難免惶恐，小黑表示，心中相當擔憂長者不願信任年輕人的想法、建議與專業；進入社區之後，才發現有所誤解，這些看著自己長大的長者，願意給予百分之百的支持，

不曾須臾懷疑。經過一段時間摸索，隨著社區營造各個計畫案推動，小黑更加確認自己的服務核心。

「人要照顧好，才能有好的傳承。」

以人作為核心，以人作為關懷，以人作為主要服務對象。各個計畫如火如荼，包含成立長青食堂、社區照顧關懷據點、巷弄長照站、牽罟文化傳承、陸蟹復育、生態導覽員培訓等。含括的子計畫，以及具體實踐方式，無不以多元活動呈現，例如環境教育課程、資源回收、淨灘、在地特色產品製作、長者鼓隊、沙地花生認養等。計畫開枝散葉，從孺子的教育培訓，到皓首的經驗分享，藉由各個活動，大幅拉近人與社區的親密度，而使每一個人，都能適切找到自己的位置與意義。

「人才是上（最）重要的。」吳季信說。

「一隻螃蟹如果沒有腳，是不會前進的。」吳誌祥說。

青年與長輩，個體與群體，過去與未來，這從來就不是一個人的故事，而是一個社區團隊相互支援的故事。我們在這裡生活，這裡是故鄉，這裡是山與海的交集，這裡是長大與終老的地方。

■■■

Profile

頭城搶孤是全臺規模最大的搶孤活動，具備超渡孤魂、慎終追遠的宗教涵意。「肉粽棧」是以肉粽為祭品，每年一千多顆肉粽動員全村才得以完成。如今，熟稔這項民俗技藝的耆老日漸凋零。

用手機掃描QR code，深入認識頭城職日生

▲ 收聽訪談

The Qianggu Festival (also known as Ghost Grappling Festival) in Toucheng is one of Taiwan's most famous and important folk traditions, where teams of competitors race to climb tall greased poles and bamboo towers

Wu Ji-sin / Wu Zhi-xiang:
Preservers of the Qianggu Culture in Gangkou, Toucheng

covered in auspicious items. The festival was originally intended to commemorate the hardships and struggles of the ancestors who crossed the Taiwan Strait to reclaim and settle in Taiwan. Facing challenges such as natural disasters, miasmas, maladies, and conflicts with other ethnic groups, many of them died without anyone noticing or knowing their whereabouts, and so became wandering spirits with nowhere to go. To honor those ancestors, appease ghosts and spirits of the deceased, and help those in need, people in Toucheng started the Qianggu Festival. Over time, it slowly evolved from a worship event to a team competition, and finally to a representative activity in Toucheng combining sports, folklore, tourism, and other cultural interpretation elements.

Wu Ji-sin, a leading figure in the Gangkou Community of Toucheng, Yilan, described the Qianggu practice in detail, including how raw materials are obtained, how to make and transport the bamboo trestlework, and related taboos. He lamented that today only a few local elders—less than ten—are familiar with this folk art.

In October 2022, he led the Gangkou Community Development Association to set up a public installation—a scaled-down version of the bamboo trestlework with glutinous rice dumplings tied to it—on the expansive lawn of the PillPEOPLE Park that was newly established in 2021 on the south side of the Gangkou coastal trail, in the hope that the public can come to a better understanding of the Qianggu practice.

In preserving cultural heritage, it is important that the elderly pass on their knowledge and skills and that young people become more involved in it. Proper care for the elderly is essential. In Gangkou, Wu Zhi-xiang, a young native of Toucheng, has made great efforts for this cause. After working in senior long-term care for years, he returned to Toucheng in 2017 to work on community development projects, as he recognized that the community was facing a serious aging problem and that the sustainability of a community required more youth involvement.

For Wu Ji-sin, Wu Zhi-xiang, and many other natives, Toucheng—located at the junction of the mountains and the sea—is their hometown, the place where they grew up, where they now live, and where they will grow old, and they want to make it a more supportive, cohesive place to reside in.

藝術工藝

海上的木質森林——

以木製浪板為志業・Neil Roe

"I live in Toucheng , I love surfing, carpentry, and living in the mountains."

Mu Surf，木製衝浪板工作室，藏身頭城梗枋更新路中的山間小路，位居山林，半隱於世，卻又在北部衝浪界擁有一定名聲。兩位主事者中，Neil 來自南非，長年定居臺灣，並以製作木製衝浪板作為志業。大學就讀產品設計，熟稔器具製程，曾從事潛水、衝浪與衝浪板製作相關工作。來到臺灣，原是為了拜訪大學朋友。一次假日，從桃園楊梅出發，開車至臺東渡假，受到東海岸的大海和山脈吸引就此留步，原先預估待三個月，延長至六個月，再延長至一年，最後決定長期居留。

已在臺灣 13 年，原居東澳 5 年，移至梗枋已有 4 年。Neil 表示，選擇頭城，是因為喜歡衝浪，梗枋山海相近，環境舒適宜人，適合不喜熱鬧愛好安靜的自己；另一方面，頭城是北部衝浪重鎮，假日聚集外地衝浪客，相當適合發展相關產業。當初為了找尋工作室，開車沿著山間小徑晃蕩，找到一間老屋。工作室由舊式 KTV 改建，當時已四到五年無人居住，相較濱海沿岸的建物，不僅租金低廉，還能擁有開闊空間。

那是一天的生活步調——六點起床，先跟狗狗

説聲早安，喝杯咖啡，想著今天要做些什麼，隨興所至，或許去做運動，或許決定再喝杯咖啡，步入工作室。八點開始工作，中間午休，直到四點或四點半再去衝浪。那是自行摸索的秩序，默然推動的軌跡，人與自然對話進而塑造的日常型態，由生活本身漸次滲透。

Neil 在頭城海邊衝浪，在山林中製作木浪板。

工作室的核心理念，在於環境友善（Eco-Friendly），具體實踐廢棄衝浪板的再生。

三個作業範疇。一，蒐集廢棄或準備淘汰的板子，拆卸表層玻璃纖維，取出內板，謹慎修訂，重新塑形。許多破損斷裂的衝浪板，內在的泡棉核心，其實具有再次利用的價值。

> 選擇頭城，一是喜歡衝浪，二是能聚集外地衝浪客，相當適合發展相關產業。

二，木頭以梧桐和西洋杉為大宗，均來自回收，藉此保護森林資源。有些是老房子拆卸的建材，有些來自木製棧板，更多的，是鋸木廠切割剩餘的木材（羅東鋸木廠切割不用的木頭，大多丟棄或焚毀）。工作室蒐集殘木，運來一綑一綑不同尺寸的木頭，先行挑揀，留下狀況良好的木材，加以清潔。木頭經過切割，整平拉直成為薄細木皮，可見原木的漂亮紋路。修訂板軌，再依木紋，詳加拼貼展現設計。上下兩塊木皮，緊密包裹泡棉核心，置放真空袋（Vacuum Bag）壓縮，再進行表層的玻璃纖維製程，塗抹環氧樹脂，完成外層即可打磨。

三，提供顧客訂製（Custom-Order）服務，或者重新塑造舊的衝浪板，給予新的生命。手工製作的

木質環保衝浪板，大約得花整整一個月，比一般衝浪板製成時間多一倍左右。

2022 年頭城老街文化藝術季「交織流動的海洋」，Neil 與書法家康潤之合作，重塑一來自南非的古老衝浪板，加之漂流木、老屋檜木梁柱等材質，重組拼湊再次新生。康潤之在衝浪板上書寫「織心知心」，代表不同地域的人跨海而來，相聚在此，友善互動深刻交流。爾後，兩位藝術家再次激起火花，是藝術形式的合作，是文化碰撞的浪花，是外來與在地的激盪，共同完成「複合媒材鑰匙圈」一系列產品，再次運用廢棄木材，製作衝浪板形木質鑰匙圈，予以書法題字。

「世界的名字是森林」，美國小說家勒瑰恩如此告誡。那被剩餘的，都有兀自光影，絕對值得更好的珍視，例如再次化為鑰匙圈、木項鍊、木耳環、木杯墊、木傢俱等。**我們在 Neil 身上看到的，是歷經沉澱打磨，才可能產生的生活態度，不僅只是廢棄衝浪板的再生，更是對於生態環境的深情關注。**

居處山脈，面向大海，世界與自然的給予盡皆在此。

■ ■ ■

Profile

從南非來到臺灣的 Neil，已在臺灣生活 13 年，他創立 Mu Surf，利用漂流木、再生木材，實踐廢棄衝浪板的再生，讓木材重生，以推廣生態友善的核心理念，並在頭城這個衝浪聖地，重新賦予衝浪板生命！

用手機掃描QR code，深入認識頭城職日生

▲ 收聽訪談

▲ 臉書粉專

"I live in Toucheng. I love surfing, carpentry, and living in the mountains."

Neil Roe:
Wooden Surfboard Maker & Co-owner of Mu Surf

Neil Roe is a wooden surfboard maker from South Africa who owns a wooden surfboard studio called Mu Surf on Gengxin Road, Toucheng Township, Yilan County. Though hidden in the mountains in the valley of Gengxin (formerly known as Gengfang), Mu Surf has gained a reputation in the northern Taiwan surfing community. As one of the two founders of Mu Surf, Neil has worked in various industries related to diving, surfing, and surfboard-making. He studied product design at university and has excellent skills in equipment manufacturing.

Neil moved to Taiwan 13 years ago and has been in Yilan for about 9 years—first living in Dong'ao, Su'ao Township for 5 years and then moving to Gengxin, Toucheng Township, where he has lived for the past 4 years. Neil chose Toucheng for its proximity to both the sea and the mountains and its comfortable and peaceful environment that suits his preference for quiet living. Furthermore, as he pointed out, Toucheng is known as an important surfing town in northern Taiwan, attracting surfers from all over Taiwan during holidays, which makes it an ideal location for the development of surfing-related industries.

The core principle of Mu Surf is to be environmentally friendly, with a focus on recycling discarded surfboards. Recognizing that the inner foam cores of many damaged or broken boards can still be utilized, Neil has repaired and brought to life many discarded surfboards. The recycling process involves collecting discarded or soon-to-be-discarded boards, disassembling the fiberglass surface, taking out the inner plate, and meticulously refurbishing and reshaping the board.

As Neil tirelessly strives to give discarded surfboards a new life, he shows not only his deep concern for the environment but also his great respect for everything that life has offered to us—something that can only be gained through years of experience.

For Neil, living in the mountains, facing the sea, with the world and nature at his doorstep, there is nowhere else he would rather be.

公眾環境

歸去來兮——

分享永續的農村生活・卓陳明

　　一面是山，一面是海，沿著北部濱海公路前行，轉向更新路，日夜淙淙流動的梗枋溪伴隨在旁。群山包圍，林木繚繞，雲霧瀰漫，這裡是創立於 1979 年的頭城休閒農場，總面積超過一百公頃，每個區域均有各自功能，包含有機蔬菜園區、果園、雞舍、牛舍、綠色廚房、烘焙窯、步道、酒莊以及各種體驗場所。自然之中，生命再次迎向本初，身體與精神彷彿從遠方賦歸。

　　遼闊的休閒農場，由一位意志堅定的女性創建。

　　卓陳明，人稱卓媽媽，老家臺中清水，出生日治末期 1940 年，自臺北女子師範學校（現為臺北市立教育大學）畢業後，擔任十年國小教職，爾後轉職為成衣廠老闆，並在 40 歲投入所有積蓄，毅然決然買下頭城梗枋山區約 80 公頃土地。一路以來，從老師、老闆至老農的歷程，輝煌成功如同傳奇。**那是對繁華文明的悖離，對農村生活的擁抱**，反璞歸真，不曾動搖，擁有過人膽量，以及對於生命的清朗見地。

　　自我擇選的生活，成為眾人歸返的原鄉。卓陳明自陳，當初積攢的錢，足足可在臺北精華地段買下大廈樓層，心中卻有另一深沉聲音：對於鄉村生活的嚮往。要當一位享受物質的文明人，或是當一

卓媽媽 40 歲時來到頭城，
毅然投入農村生活。

位夕露沾我衣的農村人？腦海浮現的，是稻田、菜
畦與果園，是流水、樹木與丘壑，是農人之間的噓
寒問暖誠摯關切，是以，順著心意來到頭城。

　　木欣欣以向榮，泉涓涓而始流，買了土地，才
發現自己什麼都不懂，得彎下脊梁，得蹲低身子，
得剪枝，得拔草，一切重新開始點滴學習。農村生
活，不僅晨興理荒穢，不僅帶月荷鋤歸，更是對於
本我、自然與生命的重新探究：如何栽培有機蔬菜，
如何面對山豬、山羌、食蟹獴與麝香貓的覓食，如
何順應氣候更易耕作，如何應對病蟲害，如何推廣
三生（生產、生活與生態結合）概念，如何再次有
效使用廢棄物——其中核心，無非是帶著生命教育

的「永續發展」。

　　一畦一畦長形有機菜園，演繹生命的循環。所生雜草供予兔子與牛隻食用，或者利用落葉披蓋土壤，使其保溫，抑制雜草。所選菜葉大多適合多雨氣候，少病蟲害，包含鳳尾 A 菜、萵苣、紅蘿蔔、芹菜、四季豆、地瓜葉、甜菜根、茼蒿、蚵白菜等。此外，牲畜排遺用作堆肥，再以養分形式滋養果園，果子成熟再度回到餐桌。農場所見，是有機，是節能減碳，是物品的循環使用，卓陳明表示，除了躬身學習新知之外，這更是老一輩傳承下來的生活態度，其內部倫理，恰恰與科學強調的永續精神不謀而合。

> 從老師、老闆至老農，
> 順著心意來到頭城，是
> 對自我的皈依。

　　頭城休閒農場提供多元面向，包含農業生產、生態導覽、手作藝術、提供在地特色食物等，對於卓陳明而言，每一位客人都如親朋好友，其最大心願，便是讓客人好好體驗農村生活，**希望藉由親身經驗，再次與自然親密互動，浸濡大地給予的生命教育**。此外，思考農場如何結合教學，同頭城四所小學合作，深根食農基礎教育；更與宜蘭大學、佛光大學等高等學院，進行長期的產學交流。

| 1 | 3 |
| 2 | |

1 頭城休閒農場提供多元面向服務。
2 蔬菜採有機種植，揀擇後不要的菜葉，可直接給牛隻加菜。
3 來農場體驗生態，學習手作，與自然親密互動。

　　歸去來兮，田園將蕪胡不歸？一位春風化雨的老師，一位叱吒商場的老闆，如今成為一位種菜養牛腳踏泥土的老農，卓陳明以她一輩子的峰迴路轉，以一整座山頭的富足豐饒，彷彿在在驗證，我們來自的地方，也終將是我們回歸的地方。

■■■

Profile

　　頭城休閒農場，創設於民國 68 年，在尊重自然，關心生態環境前提下，利用農業生產、自然生態及農村文化等資源，提供國內外遊客休閒遊憩之際，還能親身體驗農村生活。

用手機掃描QR code，
深入認識頭城職日生

▲臉書粉專

Toucheng Leisure Farm is a vast recreational farm founded by a strong-willed woman, Cho-Chen Ming, or Mrs. Cho. She grew up in Qingshui, Taichung, and after graduating from

Cho-Chen Ming: Founder of Toucheng Leisure Farm

college, she worked as an elementary school teacher for ten years and then became a clothing factory owner. At age 40, she invested all her savings in buying a piece of mountain land, approximately 80 hectares in size, in Gengxin (formerly named Gengfang), Toucheng. In 1979, she founded Toucheng Leisure Farm, covering over 100 hectares of land. The farm boasts a wide variety of facilities, spots, and trails for tourists to explore and experience, such as the organic vegetable garden area, orchards, chicken coops, water buffalo barns, the Green Kitchen area, the mud-oven baking area, the winery, and more.

Mrs. Cho voluntarily decided to establish a recreational farm in Toucheng. Following that, she committed herself to learning every aspect of the trade from scratch, rising early to till the soil and returning home at dusk with a hoe in hand and the moon as her companion. Over time, she learned how to cultivate organic vegetables, how to adjust working schedules according to weather conditions, how to deal with animal predation and pests, how to make the most of waste materials, and how to apply the farming strategies that harmonize the three aspects of production, life, and ecology. As she toiled away day in and day out, she also gained profound insights about herself, the natural world, and the very essence of life—realizing that "sustainable development" is at the core of all things.

Her farm boasts an array of rectangular organic vegetable gardens and a whole lot of designs aligning with the sustainable principles of energy conservation, carbon reduction, and material recycling, showcasing the wondrous intricacies of the cycle of life. As Mrs. Cho pointed out, the sustainable principles happen to be quite similar to the respectful attitude that the older generation holds towards nature and life.

For Mrs. Cho, her greatest wish is to provide every guest with a transcendent experience of rustic living when they come to the farm. In addition, she hopes to inspire more young minds to see the wonders of agriculture. So far, she has collaborated with four elementary schools in Toucheng to promote foundational learning in farming and food and participated in long-term industry-academia collaboration programs with universities such as National Ilan University and Fo Guang University.

Once a teacher who had nurtured countless students and a clothing factory owner who had achieved remarkable success in the industry, Mrs. Cho is now a farmer who owns a fertile farm, finding fulfillment working in her farm, spending her days cultivating crops and raising cows. Her story seems to embody the belief that we all come from nature and will return to nature in the end.

在地產業

大海的贈予
—— 以定置漁網友善海洋・張立人

東北角頭城石城，面向遼闊的太平洋，展開頎長的濱海沿岸。一日出港兩次的定置漁網捕撈船正要入港，運回漁獲——活蹦亂跳的鮮魚，正是大海不求回報的慷慨贈予。潮汐起伏，日復往返，魚隻上岸分類再予出售，部分批發至市場，部分現場散賣，部分由批發商親自取貨，魚貨量大時則送至工廠加工。

張立人，1956 年生，頭城人，現為臺灣定置漁業協會榮譽理事長。年少喜愛海釣，因緣際會接觸定置漁網，並成為畢生志業。所謂定置漁網，屬建網類，為網漁具八大類之一。在特定海域（多為礁石岩岸）敷設網具，以錨石碇、繩索、浮球、漁網等器具定著，魚群因洋流迴游自動入網，利用魚兒遇見阻礙改變方向的天性，使之滯留。**漁民不必四處追逐，只要航至架設區即可捕撈，屬於一種較為友善的被動式捕魚漁法。**

定置漁網，源自日本富山縣和石川縣一帶。日治時代引進技術，並在全臺架設大型定置網，東部沿海設置的數量甚為可觀。臺灣定置漁業協會每三個月例行開會一次，同日本石川縣定置漁網協會（姐妹會）合作，臺日兩端，每兩年輪流派員相互參訪、交流與互動。此外，為了學習新技術，臺方會

大半輩子在漁場中打拚的
張立人。

特別派遣員工至日本受訓。

　　頭城共有五處定置漁網，包含石城漁港（光榮定置漁場）、桶盤堀漁港、蕃薯寮漁港、大溪漁港和梗枋漁港，是地方上深具特色的傳統捕撈方式。定置漁網的結構可分四部分：垣網、運動場網、登網與袋網。魚群順著潮流，由垣網進入運動場網，再逐漸進入登網，最終集中左右兩側袋網。每年七月底收網，一方面躲避颱風，一方面清除附著網具的海洋生物，十月再度置放漁網。光榮定置漁場，主要以北赤道暖流黑潮的魚種為主：白帶魚、紅目鰱、鮪魚、鰆、花腹鯖、巴鰹、雙帶鰺、黃鰭鮪、鬼頭刀、日本金梭魚、紅甘、浪人鰺等。

　　一路以來不乏挑戰，不僅得確切了解潮汐、洋

流、海床地質狀態，還得面對人員培訓、行銷、技術更新、漁工凋零等諸多面向；此外，大自然始終難以精準預測。「很多情況不是自己可以控制，氣候變化往往超乎想像，例如流水不照正常運行，風浪異常破壞網具等等」。為了清楚了解現場狀況，必須躬身出海，而非坐等漁獲。隨著年歲漸增，體力漸衰，經驗與技術亦

> 利用定置漁網，使魚群因洋流迴游自動入網，漁民只需要「守網待魚」。

得傳承延續，如今，光榮定置漁場負責人已從張立人交棒給下一代。

相較傳統的捕撈方式，**定置漁網蘊含永續漁業的精神**，具有多種特徵：大幅節省漁船的高耗油航行、避免過漁及亂漁、漁獲鮮甜高利、漁民作息正常、安全性高、可統整發展為沿岸觀光漁業等，同時，對於誤入漁網的鯨鯊、海豚、玳瑁等，予以放生保護。

張立人對於畢生從事的行業，具有高度自覺，積極統整，努力朝向多角化經營。「網元漁坊」位於大里漁港南側，是複合式據點，計畫結合海鮮餐廳、咖啡廳、民宿和新鮮漁貨直銷市場，一方面帶領訪客品嘗海鮮、認識海洋，另一方面積極推廣定置漁網；此

1. 光榮定置漁場，主要以北赤道暖流黑潮的魚種為主。
2. 海面上可見定置漁網的浮球。
3. 光榮定置漁場的設置規模。

處亦曾無償提供場地，供予縣府辦理永續海洋的全縣教師研習活動等。

「魚仔鮮，就好食，拄拄（剛剛）掠起來的魚，有魚仔芳（香氣）。」張立人說起魚，如數家珍，包含命名、種類、季節、區域、生長環境、獨居群居特性、料理方式，以及魚與漁人一則一則故事。大半輩子，張立人都在漁場中打拚，在波浪中起伏，從認識海鮮到認識海洋，這一路走來，是商業與文化的水陸並進，更是對於地域環境的深度探索。

東北季風南下，一波一波鋒面來襲，肥美剽悍的魚群就要來了。

▪▪▪

Profile

「網元漁坊」位於大里漁港南側，是光榮定置漁場直營的海鮮餐廳，一方面帶領訪客品嘗海鮮、認識海洋，另一方面積極推廣定置漁網；此處亦曾無償提供場地，供予縣府辦理永續海洋的全縣教師研習活動。

用手機掃描QR code，
深入認識頭城職日生

▲臉書粉專

Zhang Li-ren, Honorary President of the Taiwan Set-Net Fishery Association, developed a passion for sea fishing from a young age. After being introduced to set-net fishing through a chance encounter, he decided

Zhang Li-ren:
Promoter of Set-Net Fishery in Toucheng

to make it his career. The so-called "set-net fishing" is a method of using set-nets—one of the most common eight fishing gears—to catch fish in specific marine areas, mostly near reefs or rocky shores. The set-net is usually anchored in place using tools such as stones, ropes, floats, and fishing nets, taking advantage of tidal movements, fish migration patterns, and the natural behavior of fish to change direction when encountering obstacles to catch fish.

Compared with traditional fishing methods,

set-net fishing is more sustainable. It can significantly reduce the envi-ronmental impact of fishing by eliminating the need for fuel-intensive fishing trips and helping to prevent overfishing. In addition, it offers other benefits such as allowing fishermen to catch fresher fish, earn higher profits, maintain regular working schedules, and work in a safer environment. It also creates opportunities for developing coastal tour-ism and makes it possible to release marine animals (e.g. whale sharks, dolphins, hawksbill turtles, etc.) that are accidentally caught in the net back into the ocean.

"Recently caught fish taste and smell fresh and sweet," said Zhang. He is extremely knowledgeable about fish, including their naming conven-tions, species, seasons, habitats, social behavior, etc., and loves talking about cooking methods and stories about fish and fishermen at length to people around him. He has spent his whole life at sea and in the fishing industry, constantly striving to deepen his understanding of ma-rine creatures, ecosystems of both sea and land, and the commercial and cultural aspects of fishing.

"When the northeast monsoon winds start to blow or when the front draws near, that means schools of big and vigorous fish are coming!" he said with great excitement.

在海上——

環保艦隊清海廢．黃士洋

　　午後，漁船切開青藍大海，波浪起伏，顛晃入港，穩穩停靠大溪漁港。船上漁工自有分屬職責，協力卸貨，一箱一箱裝滿漁獲的方型塑膠桶拉上了岸，裡頭是剛剛捕撈上岸的蝦與魚隻。魚群展鰭，蝦隻蹦跳，海水瀰漫迷人鮮甜，那彷彿是洋流的味道，是深海的容納，是生命源源不絕的起始。

　　一位曬得黝黑身著涉水褲的青年露出微笑，迎向前來。

　　黃士洋，1983 年生，龜山島移民，捕魚第三代，是土生土長的頭城人，更是「金隆勝 6 號」副船長。大學研讀企管，曾在臺北從事房仲，在臺中從事補教與廣告媒體行銷，外地闖蕩至三十歲，歸返家鄉。當時母親高血壓併發中風，需要家人協助。黃士洋放棄臺中工作，回到宜蘭帶著母親就醫，同時跟著父親出海，不知不覺慢慢承接家業。

　　這當然不是一件容易的工作，不管是從長輩身上學習技術、承襲知識，或是習慣捕魚規律且疲倦的勞動生活。一天得工作十二個小時，除非海相不佳，不然全年無休。晨早三、四點起床，摸黑出門，開船出海，徑直工作直到下午兩到三點，趕赴兩點半拍賣，緊接整理器物，或者協助攤位販售漁獲，夜間九點至十點準時就寢。

金隆勝 6 號的捕撈作業範圍，東至龜山島東側海域，南至蘭陽溪河口，魚區世代相承。早年漁獲豐富，捕撈魚蝦，然而近年暖冬，鯖魚、黑喉、白口魚、刺鯧、尖梭等魚群大幅銳減，當地漁民逐漸轉為以捕撈蝦類，作為主要的經濟來源，包含甜蝦、葡萄紅蝦、海草蝦、牡丹蝦、櫻花蝦和胭脂蝦等。

「垃圾愈來愈多，漁獲卻愈來愈少。」黃士洋捕魚十年，發出沉重感慨。

黃士洋對於大海，擁有一份誠摯的情感，**這份情感，來自面向大海的涉入、養息與相互共生，並且由此激發行動。**2022 年 1 月，同海洋發展所合作，成立大溪漁港環保艦隊，呼籲漁船共同加入（現在

黃士洋對於大海，擁有一份誠摯的情感。

已有十八艘漁船參與），帶回海廢，類別分為一般垃圾與回收物品。經由累積點數，換取洗衣粉、洗衣精和米等基本生活所需。另一方面，協調適合存放海廢的位置，讓相關的回收工作，不致產生額外負擔。因其行動，獲頒當年度全國績優環保艦隊之「最佳艦隊獎—優等獎」。

> **一天工作十二個小時，**
> **卻發現漁獲越來越少，**
> **垃圾越來越多。**

同時，成立臉書「阿洋船長的海廢日誌」，透過自己的漁船視野，讓更多人看到海洋，認識海洋——那是浩瀚豐美，亦是塑化垃圾的漂浮遺棄。黃士洋指出，希望大溪漁港成為一處海廢回收的「示範港」，**更希望藉由海廢照片的分享，喚醒更多人對於海洋生態的關注，進而達到「源頭減塑」，讓大海與漁業能夠永續發展。**這些積極作為，無疑就是「行動呼籲」（Call to Action）的最佳示範。

2006 年，一份由海洋生態學家鮑里斯·沃姆（Boris Worm）主導的國際合作海洋報告指出，由於人類濫捕與水質汙染，若不採取積極行動，到了 2048 年，所有經濟性魚類及海產生物都會枯竭，海洋生態將澈底崩解，汪汪大海無蝦無魚。我們尚未能夠確認預警是否真會實現，但可以知曉，海洋生

1	2
3	4

1 漁船入港，帶回魚蝦與海廢。
2 他對海廢展開行動，並獲得環保艦隊優等獎的獎盃。
3 上岸後立刻處理魚貨。
4 近年來「捕」到的海廢無奇不有。

物確實正在大量削減。作為第一線的見證者，黃士洋不僅只是記錄、擔憂，更以自己的行動，努力影響身邊的親友、社區與整個社會。

那一張帶著紋路的笑臉，踏上甲板，踏上浪，同時踏上人類與自然共享的命運。

■ ■ ■

Profile

黃士洋祖輩是龜山島子民，後遷居大溪仁澤社區，世代以捕魚維生，30 歲那年決定返鄉，靠海吃海。希望以漁民的親身體驗，喚醒社會大眾關心日益嚴重的海洋汙染，致力海洋生態環境保護。

用手機掃描QR code，深入認識頭城職日生

▲ 收聽訪談　　▲ 臉書粉專

Huang Shi-yang, a native of Toucheng, was born into a family of fishermen. His ancestors originally resided in Guishan Island (Turtle Island) and later relocated to the Renze

Huang Shi-yang:
Sea Captain Dedicated to Marine Protection

Community in Toucheng. Today, as the third generation of fishermen in his family, he is the deputy captain of the "Jin Long Sheng No. 6" fishing boat. But he did not start his career as a fisherman. He studied business administration in college and had worked in the real estate and tutoring industries in Taipei and media advertising/marketing in Taichung for a few years before returning to Toucheng at age 30, when his mother suffered a stroke due to complications from high blood pressure. After returning home, Huang balanced caring for his mother with gaining practical knowledge and expertise in fishing. He went on fishing trips with his father and consulted frequently with experienced fishermen, gradually taking over the family business and getting used to the tiresome and mundane routine of fishing.

Fishing is a very demanding job, with working hours typically extending up to 12 hours a day and no breaks throughout the year, unless the ocean is not safe because of the bad weather. Having spent a considerable amount of time around the ocean, Huang has developed a profound emotional bond and a mutually beneficial relationship with it, which has inspired him to initiate actions to protect the sea.

In January 2022, he collaborated with the Marine and Fisheries Development Office of Yilan County to establish the Daxi Fishing Port environmental protection fleet, which now consists of 18 fishing boats. The mission of the fleet is to reduce marine waste, and the fishermen who bring back the marine waste—both general waste and recyclable materials—can earn points and later redeem them for daily supplies such as laundry detergent and rice. The waste brought back is properly taken to and stored at suitable locations, thanks to Huang's efforts in coordinating with relevant individuals and units.

With a bright smile on his wrinkled face, Huang once again steps onto the deck and sets sail to start fishing, while at the same time embarking on a journey to protect the ocean and the harmonious coexistence between humans and nature.

帶路人
講故事

黎萬青

非常受歡迎的
老街導覽員，為
遊客述說家鄉
的美，開啓生命
與土地的連結。

大自然的創造、山海交界的關口

北關海潮公園，又稱為蘭城公園，被列為蘭陽八景之一。位於頭城濱海公路旁，美麗的景色經常吸引來往遊客們駐足，最大的特色就是園內林立的礁岩，海岸邊佇立著歷經千萬年沖刷而成的單面山、豆腐岩、小海岬等自然石岩景觀，在巨石與山勢之間設有階梯，山壁間的夾縫處透入微光，形成獨特的「一線天」奇景，站在其間，海風輕輕拂過，暖暖的陽光灑落，不妨停下來，享受片刻的歲月靜好。

沿著步道而上，一路蜿蜒到觀海涼亭，可以聽濤、遠眺龜山島，這裡是最接近龜山島的陸地區域，等一等還能看到火車跑過！

千百年來海蝕所形成的地質風貌，可以見到一面傾斜，一面陡峻的單面山和岩壁插入海面，岩壁與海浪相激盪，捲起白濤響浪，自古便有「蘭城鎖鑰扼山腰，雪浪飛騰響怒潮」的名句，形容北關海潮澎湃壯闊的景致。

　　北關海潮公園內設有兩尊古砲，滿清時期，這裡是防止盜匪進入宜蘭的最佳關隘，因此設立駐兵關卡，嘉慶年間，設立兩座砲台，距今已有 160 多年的歷史，為北關增添了不少古風遺韻。

　　豐富的地質景觀，橫看成嶺側成峰，因為海與風，石群千萬年來不曾停止變化，這是海蝕的痕跡，歲月的刻印。（口述／黎萬青，文字／楊宇伶）

1. 黎萬青推薦大家驅車離開市區，往北關一遊。**2.** 這裡是離龜山島最近的陸地。**3.** 砲台古蹟訴說此地過往的軍事重要性。（圖片提供：黎萬青）**4.** 登高俯瞰，看見白浪拍岸，火車穿梭。

山與海的職日生：頭城職人誌

作　　　者／連明偉

英　　　譯／李婉如

編　　　輯／楊宇伶

協 力 編 輯／葛晶瑩

總 　編 　輯／彭仁鴻

發 　行 　人／彭仁鴻

出 版 發 行／蘭城巷弄有限公司

　　　　　　宜蘭縣 261 頭城鎮中庸街 32 號　電話：0911220886

　　　　　　E-mail：yilanane@gmail.com

　　　　　　FB：https://www.facebook.com/goldfishspace

帶路人文字／簡云開、楊宇伶

影　　　像／曠辰昕、游庭軒、令和創意

插畫與地圖／亮亮

封 面 設 計／林曉涵

內 頁 排 版／林曉涵

印　　　刷／長順印刷事業有限公司

2023 年 5 月 20 日 初版一刷 Printed in Taiwan

定價 499 元

▲ Line 官方帳號　　▲臉書專頁

國家圖書館出版品預行編目資料

山與海的職日生：頭城職人誌/連明偉著. -- 宜蘭縣頭城
鎮：蘭城巷弄有限公司, 2023.05
　面；　公分.
　ISBN 978-626-97428-0-6(平裝)

1.CST：人文地理 2.CST：歷史 3.CST：宜蘭縣頭城鎮

733.9/107.9/117.4　　　　　　　　112007333